What Othe...

Joy Fueled has achieved what few books in our time have done—restoring healthy motivation that grows people who respond like Jesus would. Relational joy is the energy behind all healthy and godly growth. Instead of being beat up by another vision of what we should do, readers are welcomed into a contagious expression of life. Discover what joy can do!

Dr. Jim Wilder - Clinical Psychologist & Neurotheologian, author, international speaker who develops ways to apply brain science to Christian practices that transform us into the character of Christ. He helps existing relational networks build joy, suffer well, love enemies and grow a mature community with the resilience to overcome trauma under the guidance of Christ's Spirit.

*****

The folks at LK10 are tapping into some ideas and practices that have the potential to revolutionize how people experience Christ-based community in their lives. At the center of this is relationship — not the distant, austere, duty-based perspective common in many religious systems, but rather vital, communicative, authentic connections with Christ and each other, relationships that spawn joy and transformation. I especially appreciate how their practical, hands-on emphasis, strongly influenced by current psychology and brain science, is an outflow of a theology deeply rooted in the love of God.

Steve Adams - Founder of LivingFORward and author of *Sacred Intersections: Enjoying and Enhancing the Stories Around Us.* (www.livingFORward.us)

*****

The church in the West is in decline because faith, as it has been predominantly shared and practiced, simply doesn't work. *Joy Fueled* testifies to an experiential life with God, rooted in scripture and neural science, that addresses the deepest needs of the human heart. This important and ground breaking book has the potential to radically change how we make disciples and create community in the way of Jesus in the 21st century.

Mark Scandrette - Adjunct professor, Fuller Theological Seminary, and author of *Practicing the Way of Jesus, FREE* and *Belonging and Becoming*.

*****

You are going to enjoy this book! John, Toni, and Kent draw us back to the source and meaning of joy, and it is not what you have learned. Joy is about being rightly connected to God and it results in our being on his mission in a community of joy fueled Christ-followers. As the authors say, "It is out of God's deep desire to enjoy us fully that he ignites our heart for the world." If you are tired of searching for joy by doing good things, this book will renew your hope in the Holy Spirit who fuels you with joy as you live in community as the Bride.

Michael T. Cooper - Missiologist and author of *Ephesiology: The Study of the Ephesian Movement*.

*****

Having grown up in a Jewish family where everyone was always talking but no one was listening, I have found that the principles of LK10 fulfill a great need in the Jewish world - to learn to actively listen while others are speaking and to operate out of joy, not fear nor guilt. Also, I deeply appreciate how the people at

LK10 respect Biblical Judaism and the Hebrew language. When my people Israel adopt gratitude instead of kvetching, become joy-fueled Ima's and Aba's and learn the wisdom from LK10 teachings, we will then be prepared to declare Matthew 23:39: "Baruch Haba b'Shem Adonai," and see the return of our Messiah Yeshua!

Carolyn Margolin-Hyde - Founder of Heart of G-d Ministries, singer/songwriter.

*****

An insightful, inspirational and encouraging book for those who are tired of running on the "low grade fuels of duty, obligation and guilt!" Offers real and concrete solutions for leaders who long to see the "spontaneous expansion" of the church! A feeling of hope leaps off the pages!

John Porter - House to House Ministries.

*****

As one who has been in church all his life, I understand the increasing number of Christians who are "done" with church. At the same time, Jesus and the early Christians are clear that one needs a community to maintain trust in Jesus. But what should this community/church/fellowship look like? The authors of *Joy Fueled* point us away from questions of church structure and mission method to the heart of church. Through rest, quiet, and listening we experience the joy we cannot contain, the joyous good news of relationship with God that we spontaneously share with others.

Gary Holloway, Ph.D. - Executive Director of World Convention and author of *Living God's Love: An Invitation to Christian Spirituality.*

*****

A growing literature is analyzing, interpreting and strategizing responses to the phenomenon of those variously referred to as 'church leavers', 'post-church', 'church refugees' or 'dones'. What *Joy Fueled* offers is its distinctive focus on a spirituality marked by joy rather than obligation, delight rather than duty. This is refreshing and crucial.

Stuart Murray Williams, Ph.D. - Freelance trainer/consultant with the Anabaptist Network, and coordinator of Urban Expression, a pioneering church planting agency. He is the author of *Church Planting, Post Christendom* and *Church After Christendom*

*****

We are created for relationships. Specifically, joyful relationships where we are glad to be together. *Joy Fueled* gives a refreshing and invigorating vision for the transformative journey where God's people can become a forest of trees planted near rivers of living water. Picking up this book will inspire, motivate and compel you to pursue the kind of life defined by, you got it, joy! Throw off the guilt and shame to discover a new motivator for life and community. You will not want to put this book down – or keep it to yourself!

Chris Coursey - President of THRIVEtoday (thrivetoday.org), an organization focused on interactive training in the 19 relational skills so God's people are fully equipped to make relationships work. Chris is an international speaker, curriculum designer and author of 9 books focusing on relational skills for families and communities.

*****

Perhaps the number one reason "Dones" tell me they have left church, is the loss of joy in their experience of church. Instead of church being a joyful community that empowers meaningful life, it has become for them a flat, listless routine, or all too often, an organization that mimics an addicted, anxious, abusive, shame-based family. This volume offers wisdom from spiritual giants, ministry pioneers, and science to help missional leaders and new forms of faith community live with the joy of the Lord as their strength.

Elaine A. Heath, Ph.D. - President, Neighborhood Seminary

*****

A refreshing reminder that joy awaits, renews, and restores followers of Jesus; that gratitude and relationship provide a welcome salve to duty and isolation. The authors of *Joy Fueled* gently redirect mission to its origin—the formation of the gospel within us as it blooms in joy.

Monty Lynn, Ph.D. - Professor of Management, Abilene Christian University

*****

In my role as a church planter and denominational leader for the past 34 years, I have seen the need to move beyond what we experience in our current church structures. *Joy Fueled* offers a way to help lead a community of believers into a deeper, heart-level relationship with Jesus and others. I believe that the relational pathways written about in this book will help create the new wineskins the church so desperately needs.

Mike Hoffmann - Baptist Association Mission Strategist

*****

What is the source? What is the fuel? Face to face relational joy and attachment. That is what we all cry for because that is what we were made for. There are three basic needs of every human heart.

Identity (Who am I?)
Belonging (Who are my people?)
Purpose (What am I created for?)

There is a desperate desire in the global Body and Bride of Christ for authentic relationship and Christ-like transformation. *Joy Fueled* trumpets an incisive, simple and practical response to these needs. It's an invitation into the reality of joyful, vibrant, spiritual family. As a husband, father and pastor who highly values authentic community and transformation, I was privileged to discover Luke 10 and my friends John, Kent and Toni. We together share a passion for joy-fueled, Jesus-led micro community that is often missing in both institutional and house church settings. After 8 years of applying this "fuel" in our local church community, as well as internationally with artists, missionaries and nationals, I can say with confidence, "It works!" Relational joy is truly the high octane fuel of the Kingdom!

Kent Larson - Pastor of Pastoral Care Vineyard Community Church (https://vcchurch.com), Director of Mercy Transformation Center (https://mercytransformation.com/) Laguna Niguel, CA Founder of Mercy Arts (mercyarts.org/) and The Artist Circle network.

*****

John, Toni, and Kent from LK10 challenge us to examine the ways we think and talk about God's invitation to join him in his mission. I read this book while on a trip in Poland inviting believers to join with us in providing access to God's Word to every language group. The insights provided led me to shift my language from that of duty and obligation and focus on joy and opportunity. Finding joy in our relationships and our ministries begins, as the authors point out, with understanding that God takes joy in us--not in our works or successes, but in us as his beloved children. As I prepare new missionaries from around the world, this one insight could relieve much of the anxiety that many feel as they respond to God's call.

Anthony Parker - D. Min. - Leads the Global Partnerships Division and serves as a coach in the Formation Department at Pioneer Bible Translators. He is also an adjunct professor of intercultural studies at Johnson University.

*****

Liberating reading. I loved it: a balm for us duty-driven work slaves. Joy in the power of God's Holy Spirit is the attractive "missional" energy the Biblical testimony teaches.

Charles L. Harper, Jr. - D. Phil., cosmologist, theologian and Sunday-school teacher, former Executive Director of the John Templeton Foundation

*****

In 1991, convinced that what we called church was not what I found in my Bible, my wife and I left the traditional church and moved across the country to start over with people who didn't know us, to live among the lost and be salt, light and a fragrant aroma. We tried joining some house gatherings, but it was like the big box church in a little box.

Where was this book then? Well, it's here now and I'm thankful. *Joy Fueled* is the most practical how-to book on building deep and meaningful spiritual community you will read. John, Toni and Kent have made it simple for anyone to build relationship-based, transformative spiritual community in their living room, and do it with joy.

Chuck Blakeman - Started and built ten businesses in the U.S., Europe, and Africa. He is the founder of Crankset Group and 3 to 5 Clubs, providing business advisory for leaders and companies worldwide.

*****

Joy Fueled is a must read for anyone in ministry/church leadership who is looking for a more life giving, unburdened way to do ministry and live as a Jesus follower. When I learned how to be fueled by joy in my life and work, everything began to change, from my relationship with my husband, to how I lead my coworkers, and to how I teach and interact with college students. Lk10 and the concepts in this book have brought transformation and multiplication in unprecedented ways, as I have learned to let "Jesus do the heavy lifting." I am forever grateful to John, Toni, and Kent.

Colleen Caskey - Mid-Atlantic Regional Coordinator for Athletes Ministry in InterVarsity

*****

I can't think of a more timely and relevant book for the American church today than this one. *Joy Fueled* shines a light on the dreary, duty-driven system that's wearing us out and provides a pathway for simple, vibrant, Jesus-led communities. It's one of those books that will be worn out from reading and sharing and reading again.

Kristen LaValley - Writer, online story teller

*****

The idea of joy, fueled by love, as a motivation for our daily work and lives? The thought gives me chills. *Joy Fueled* is like a pair of glasses, or a treasure hunt: as we read and consider, we suddenly find God everywhere, offering us joy in him! As a cancer survivor, children's musician and daughter of God, I plan to keep this book, rife with scripture, well-founded hope and wisdom, at the ready.

Katy Bowser Hutson - Member of Rain for Roots and author of *Now I Lay Me Down To Fight*

*****

Joy Fueled helps us reimagine and simplify, with grace and ease, the overly complex definitions of church so many of us now find entangled into our Christian DNA. This mutated DNA doesn't seem to be regenerating correctly anymore. In *Joy Fueled*, we are relieved of guilt, shame, debilitating duty, and compulsive knowledge-grabbing while being invited into depths of freedom, relationship, and joy. Ultimately, this book invites us to relocate our heads more deeply into our hearts. As we connect with God and others from the heart space, we discover a joy that not only fuels faith but may actually begin to heal our spiritual DNA.

Matt Wallace - Executive Director of Dry Bones Denver (drybonesdenver.org). Dry Bones is a relational ministry and community among youth and young adults experiencing houselessness in Denver, CO.

*****

More than any other book I've read in a long while, *Joy Fueled* has opened my heart in fresh ways to the real option of exchanging my hard-earned exhaustion for the rest Jesus gladly gives.

Joy Fueled gently but relentlessly exposes the plausible ways we promote dutiful productivity over relational joy as the baseline of life and service.

This book is a compelling witness to the power of simple attention-focusing rhythms of checking in with each other and listening to Jesus - power to practice ancient imperatives to love God, neighbor, and enemy in ways informed by the Holy Spirit and by current brain science.

Ian Shelburne, Ph.D. - Director of Development, Eden Center for Regenerative Culture

*****

"There has to be more." So often this is the sentiment of those who are done with the church or never connect with Christ's beautiful church in the first place. Yet the authors of *Joy Fueled* have given powerful language and validation to the "more" of God's church... namely the reclaimed and spontaneous fuel of joy that comes in relational, intimate community with others and the Triune God. As a practitioner of a church seeking to live into the "more" through a gathered and sent model of church, I find *Joy Fueled* to give refreshing and empowering language to what we desire to experience as the church but do not always know how to verbalize. Reading this book leaves me wanting to proclaim, "See...There is more! And here it is!" Any church seeking "the more" it intuitively knows is there but does not always know how to express it or experience it will benefit from this book.

Rev. Dr. Matthew E. Lake, D. Min - Lead Pastor of the First United Methodist Church of Williamsport, PA, a gathered and sent congregation. Mission strategist and trainer with Fresh Expressions U.S.

If joy is like oxygen, an indispensable factor that provides strength and energy to our most important relationships—with God, others, and even ourselves—then this book is a big deep breath, with a smile going out on the exhale. Both heartening and doable, it shows us how to cultivate the kind of joy the world is yearning to experience; the kind of joy Jesus, himself, welcomes us to know fully.

James Henderson - Co-founder, Ashrei Center for Spiritual Formation, Mexico City; a graduate of the Renovaré Institute for Christian Spiritual Formation and doctoral candidate in Spiritual Direction at Fuller Theological Seminary.

*****

Once I began reading Joy-Fueled one evening I pushed on till about 2:30 am when I was done. I realized the book was well-tuned to what my spirit needed for my own spiritual revival in a dry and burdened time. After reading it, I started meeting joy in all kinds of places I'd forgotten about.

Joy Fueled, with its reminders of the pathways to joy and God's desire for us to be filled to overflowing with the joy of the Trinity, has been good news for me and for those I have shared its insights with. I recommend this book with its focus on the infinitely renewable resource of God's joy, and am eager to see it published along with the books that will follow in the series.

David Janzen - Author of *The Intentional Christian Communities Handbook* and the founding catalyst for the Nurturing Communities Network.

*****

Jesus said, "These things I have spoken to you, that my joy may be in you, and that your joy may be full." Yet we so often settle for far less than what he offers. Joy-fueled is simple and practical for those seeking to live as followers of Jesus in whichever community they may find themselves. In the words of the authors, "God is inviting us into deep delight...." But that journey is one of starting small, being vulnerable, remaining present together in the face of conflict, and learning to listen to God, each other, and ourselves. The invitation is always there, and their words encourage any of us to dive back into life with Jesus and with one another as his disciples.

Cyrus Eaton - Dean of Spiritual Formation | Campus Chaplain, Abilene Christian University

*****

Toni, John and Kent are forging renewed life-giving relational pathways rooted in ancient Scripture for followers of Jesus to explore together. Our ways of being and doing church have worn thin in the experience of many sincere believers. The Body of Christ across the world in our day is desperate for an infusion of much more authentic love, joy, peace and resilience. The LK10 network is pioneering fresh and creative ways to inspire more robust spiritual, relational and emotional intelligence within our communities of faith. I, for one, cheer them on in their holy experiment to help pioneer and normalize a more relationally vibrant and wise approach to our discipleship to Jesus Christ. *Joy Fueled: Catalyzing a Revolution of Joy* is a valuable resource for the whole Body of Christ. With just a little prayer and creativity, many of their ideas and practices are transferable to churches of all kinds and could foster a Jesus-centric relational revolution of joy in the church and culture.

Pastor Michael Sullivant - CEO Life Model Works

Joy Fueled

Catalyzing a Revolution of Joyful Communities

John C. White   Toni M. Daniels   Dr. Kent Smith

COPYRIGHT

Joy Fueled
Catalyzing a Revolution of Joyful Communities

ISBN: 978-1-7346840-1-8

Editing and Layout by Jim Bryson (JamesLBryson@gmail.com)

Proofreading by Tammy Lancaster

65 million people in the US are done with church, and many more worldwide.

This book is for them.

Dedication

FOR THE SPIRITUAL MOMS AND DADS around the world training in the LK10 Community who are part of our communities of practice called "Leader Teams." Your stories of joy-fueled transformation in your own lives and in the lives of the people around you are daily evidence that a true revolution of joy is underway. You have been experiencing church with us and training in how to be vibrant families of Jesus and how to train others to be the same. Our hope is to give you the language you need to effectively pass on our values to third and fourth generations.

This book is also for the 65 million "Dones" and "Almost Dones" in the United States alone, and many more internationally. These are people who were once part of a church, often as leaders, pastors or missionaries, but who have left the institution and do not plan to return (*Church Refugees: Sociologists reveal why people are DONE with church but not their faith,* Packard and Hope). For you, we aim to renew your hope in what church could be and give you a pathway towards a life fueled by joy.

Table of Contents

Acknowledgements xxi

Our Beginnings xxv

Foreword xxvii

Introduction xxxi

1 A Journey of Joy 1

2 Joy 5

3 Guilt or Joy? 9

4 Inferior Fuel 15

5 What Fuels You? 23

6 Joy Fuel 35

7 The Ultimate Fuel 41

8 In The Beginning 45

9 Persistent Joy 49

10 Joy Defined 59

11 Rest and Quiet 69

12 Vibrant Families of Jesus 79

13 Joy Internal 95

14 Spontaneous Joy-Fueled Revolution 109

15 A Story to Join 117

Recommended Resources for Further Growth 123

About the Authors 133

Acknowledgements

From All of Us:

This book was in no way a one-person show, nor did it happen in a vacuum. We are deeply indebted to our families, as well as our LK10 community for the support and encouragement to put these thoughts into written form. Here are a few of those we would like to specifically thank:

The LK10 oversight and operations teams who not only heard endless talk of this book for over a year, but prayed, listened on our behalf and held us through to its completion.

Our Leader Team Pre-readers who were the first eyes on the manuscript and the feedback voices that made it better: Carolyn Hyde, John Shaw, Nigel Carson, Barbara Hoffman, Joe Showalter, Larry Silver, Ian Shelburne, Bart Moyers, Stephen Johnson, Tony Carey, Marty Uhler, Colleen Caskey.

Hilary Kline, our Book Launch Champion, rallied the troops and organized everything from creating a launch page to assuring the most successful launch possible. Her passion for "as many people as possible" to hear this message is inspiring. She could not have done this without Zach LaValley and Susan Ramsey's support as well. Thank you all!

Our proofreader, Tammy Lancaster, slaved over this book not once but twice!

Jim Bryson, our editor, and the biggest surprise! His straightforward, comedic feedback made editing a joy. Working with his suggestions definitely took this book up a notch forcing us to clarify, reduce, and even reorganize so that the reader experiences the book with the heart, not just the mind. We can't wait to work with Jim again. Thank you for your dedication to making this the best it could be.

And finally, our launch team worked hard so that a revolution of joyful communities can become a global reality. Suzanne K. Baity, Jenny Belle McCullagh, Neil Bradshaw, Lindsey Buchholz, Jordan Bunch, Tony G. Carey, Colleen Caskey, Matthew Daniels, Sandy Fitzpatrick, Kimberly Harris, Michael Harris, Katie Hartman, Barbara Hoffmann, Mike Hoffmann, Jonathan Johnson, Kent Larson, Zach LaValley, John R. Loppnow, Denice MacKenzie, Atara McGill, Ryan Nenaber, Ryan Paterson, Dennis Podryadchikov, Susan Ramsey, Larry Silver, Dan Swan, Travis Woronowicz.

Your faith is inspiring!

John:

I especially want to thank three important women in my life who have encouraged me, prayed for me and believed in me. Without them, there would be no LK10 Community and no Joy Fueled book. My wife of 30 years, Tamela. My mother of 72 years, Mary Nelson White. My daughter, Susan (Margee) Ramsey of 46 years. I love and appreciate all of you. Finally, my CO2 partner (you will learn about "Church of Two" in the book) and loyal friend, Jim Mellor, with whom I've done a "check in" almost every day for 15 years. Jim, you kept telling me I should write a book. Well, here it is!

Toni:

Thank you, Matt Daniels, for being my sounding board, think tank and sparring partner. Thank you also, for caring for our precious children many nights so that I could work on this project. We have fought for joy in every season of our life together be it in abundance and celebration or addiction and trauma. I am thankful for the grace to always find our way back to each other, and the joy that overflows to those around us.

Kent:

I have been blessed to experience Joy-Fueled community on many levels, each of which has had a vital role in forming me for this writing project: My amazing parents, Dale and Mary Jo Smith who at 88 and 90 continue to radiate love-infused joy; My beautiful and strong bride Karen with whom I share 5 children and 11 grandchildren and the ongoing adventure of nurturing a family; Our extended family, the Eden Community--a relentless source of hope and joy as we explore the contours of a vibrant family of Jesus in our time; and my friends, students and colleagues at Abilene Christian University with whom I have had the privilege over 30 years of testing and refining the ideas and practices in these books. In each case, I have found the gifts of love and joy--and I am grateful!

Our Beginnings

JOHN WHITE AND KENT SMITH MET IN 2003 while working with the U.S. branch of DAWN, a church planting organization that sought to "Disciple A Whole Nation" (DAWN). Both men were captivated by the huge vision of fulfilling the Great Commission by seeing a church in close reach of every person in every region and people group in the world.

Matt and Toni Daniels had been church planting in Uruguay, South America for 18 years. Aptly named the "graveyard of missions," Uruguay was in desperate need of an expression of church that could counter mental-illness by nurturing healthy interpersonal relationships.

After DAWN ended, John and Kent started The LK10 Community to connect and equip emerging church leaders around the world. They chose the name LK10 for Luke, chapter 10, where Jesus focuses on training and sending his disciples to start small, family-like Kingdom communities in what he calls "houses of peace" (Luke 10:5-7).

In 2013, Matt and Toni met John White. After learning of LK10's Rhythms of Attention, they knew their search for a sustainable and yet viral way of "being church" had come to an end and their hope in catalyzing a joy-fueled revolution of Jesus had begun. A year later, Toni was helping rewrite LK10's training modules to include the brain science behind the training and quickly became LK10's Training Champion.

In November of 2018, the three of them met together in Nashville for four days to forge the five core values already practiced by the LK10 Community. Emerging from those meetings was a plan for a book about each core value, beginning with Joy Fueled.

Reading a book written by three people of various backgrounds and personalities can be challenging. "Who wrote this part? Who is speaking here?" That is why the authors have tried to speak with one voice wherever possible. However, as you will note, each has unique stories to tell and therefore, you will occasionally see a particular piece credited to an author.

The concept of joy, that of being glad to be together no matter what, is the source of all the good found within these pages.

May Jesus' revolution of joy that he initiated over 2,000 years ago live on and fuel his people in all that they are and do for the Kingdom of God.

Foreword

WHEN I FIRST HEARD ABOUT the astonishing number of people who were claiming to have no religious affiliation, the "Nones," I knew there was another side to that story. Some of my previous research had introduced me to a group of people who still claimed their religious identity, but just couldn't bear to bring themselves to an institutional church anymore for one reason or another. I started referring to this group of people as the "Dones," and while I suspected that there were many more of them than anyone had previously imagined, I was shocked at what I learned.

The number of Dones in this country alone is astounding, and it speaks to a larger cultural shift that we are experiencing in America right now. As much as people want to tell the story of the Nones and Dones through a specifically religious lens, the truth is that it's a much broader issue than that. People aren't just leaving religious institutions; they're leaving ALL institutions.

A quick look at the data for institutional trust by Gallup, Pew or other reputable research institutes and academics confirms that for the last 30 years, trust in basic social institutions has been eroding. Organized religion isn't the story, in other words, it's a character in a larger narrative. People have lost trust in financial institutions, education institutions, the media and most acutely, the government, along with religion.

The difference, however, lies in the response. Each of these other sectors have made significant adaptations. Home schooling and charter schools have seen a dramatic rise as trust in public education has diminished. People have turned to smaller, local business as much as they have looked to Amazon and Wal-Mart.

Populist politicians have captured the public imagination in place of traditional candidates in both parties.

Those in the religious sector on the other hand, have been slower to take part in these innovations. While other sectors of American life have filled the trust gap with a turn toward smaller, more local, participative and conversational ways of engaging with one another, institutional religion in this country largely looks the way that it did when institutional trust was high and could be reasonably assumed.

What is desperately needed are new models, ways of thinking and innovation. I take heart and comfort in knowing that innovation is at the core of the foundations of religion in this country, but it pains me to see that we have lost this spirit in recent decades. I see young people, Nones, Dones and others who are largely unserved by current religious institutions that are stuck using models that were wildly effective once upon a time but have very little value in this new landscape. They're crying out for connection, for belonging, for community, for a safe space to explore, doubt, ask questions and be with each other.

The innovation that the church needs will not come from a single source, but from many efforts that respond to local, contextualized conditions in people's own communities. This is what brings me to *Joy Fueled*. The tools and perspectives contained in the following pages are a kind of map for how to navigate this new terrain where a one-size-fits-all approach no longer works. Getting to the heart motivation of connection, belonging, and participation, the authors present a hopeful paradigm that could lead to the type of effective innovation the church needs. Unlike some other ministry books, this one doesn't promise to have all the answers, but it will help you ask the right questions. And in an era of institutional distrust, that's about the most valuable thing one can do.

According to my research, there are over 65 million Americans who are done with church... this book is for them.

Josh Packard, Ph.D.
Executive Director
Springtide Research Institute

Introduction

ACCORDING TO A TEAM OF RESEARCHERS led by Joshua Packard and Ashleigh Hope, sixty-five million Americans, over a third of all adults in the U.S., are done with church. Millions more, though they occasionally fill a pew, are almost done. (Packard, Josh and Hope, Ashleigh. *Church Refugees: Sociologists reveal why people are DONE with church but not their faith.* Loveland, CO: Group, 2015, p. 20)

Long before LK10 began in 2008, we had been observing a great exodus from churches. We saw and felt firsthand the pain of this trend in local churches and realized the reasons people were leaving went beyond surface issues such as worship style or mission focus to more systemic issues facing both the church and society at large.

We also observed that many of the people leaving their legacy church were headed for someone's living room, a coffee shop or a street ministry. "If we can just meet more simply," we often heard, "you know, where we can practice the 'one anothers'—love one another, bear one another's burdens—like the early church, we'll finally have the church we need." Others used more missional language, "If we just get serious about loving the poor and seeing justice done and caring for the good creation God gave us, we'll have the church God intended."

All too often, that hoped-for church experience did not happen. People accustomed to a lifetime of church as a "service" employing the skills of professional teachers, worship leaders and finely-tuned programming for everything from child-care to marriage enrichment, now found themselves in meetings with none of the above. Amateur teaching, worse "worship," and no child-care, sometimes accompanied by commitments to social justice that were simply unsustainable, often led to burn out and further disillusionment.

House church in many ways was like that movie in the '80s: *Honey, I Shrunk the Kids*, only this time it was, *Honey, I Shrunk the Church*! Not much about church culture was changed except the location (and sometimes the coffee was better). Unfortunately, this experiment moved many of these people within a year or two, deeper into the "Dones" category with a firm assertion that they had, "been there, done that." And while a few of these people reluctantly made their way back to a conventional church, many more moved toward the "Nones," what social scientists call people with no religious affiliation at all.

In sharp contrast to all this church-leaving, Jesus described what it is like to actually find God's Kingdom. He said it is like a man walking through a field who discovers a great treasure. In his great joy, the man sells everything he had in order to possess it.

We have to wonder—where is that kind of Kingdom discovery happening in our time? Where is the vibrant, joy-fueled life Jesus offered so clearly on display that those who stumble across it want in, whatever the cost? And how could that opportunity be made available to everyone?

With these questions before us, in 2008, John and Kent began a networking and equipping organization called "LK10." Since then, we have been asking, "How can we do our part—no more and no less—to see a vibrant family of Jesus in close reach of everyone worldwide?" This question has challenged us from the beginning to set our attention on what we know has God's attention—the formation of a bride made up of people from all the nations of the world. We have made this our vision because we have read to the end of the Bible, and are persuaded that the vision of the great celebration of joy ahead is meant to begin now.

As we come to understand our part in this great story, we are drawn to the deep need for spiritual moms and dads who live from the joy-fueled life of God, and who are able to welcome others into these vibrant families of Jesus. But what, exactly, is a vibrant family of Jesus, and how do we find, form and empower the spiritual parents who can nurture such families?

Jesus faced precisely the same challenge as he initiated a new age of God's reign on earth. And we've seen that we won't find a better plan for raising up vibrant, joyful communities of God's life and purpose than what Jesus called his first disciples into as described in the early Christian writings. Among these, the gospel of Luke, chapter 10, offers an especially clear picture of what Jesus taught and practiced in launching these vibrant Kingdom families, the first expressions of God's Kingdom-community centered on Jesus.

Over many years of discovering how Jesus continues to form such communities in our time, we have identified five core values vital to this process. We summarize them in this packed sentence:

LK10 is a network of joy-fueled, Jesus-led communities of practice, equipping spiritual parents to nurture ecosystems of grace.

While quite a mouthful, this sentence incorporates our five core values as an organization:

- Joy Fueled
- Jesus Led
- Ecosystems of Grace
- Spiritual Mothers and Fathers
- Communities of Practice

This book, *Joy Fueled*, is the first of five planned books, each designed to unpack one of the five core values of the LK10 Community. We want to address the big question behind our vision: What would a vibrant family of Jesus, a Jesus-led church really look like? And how does Jesus call us to nurture them?

These are bold questions because they represent our belief that the church as we have known it, in significant ways, is a departure from the church that Jesus had in mind. All too often, the church that people experience is so far from the gospel (the good news) that millions have left and more are following them.

But we have solid evidence that this does not have to be the case. We have stories to tell, from across North America and around the world, that vibrant families of Jesus are alive and well today. When people follow the simple guidance of Jesus as seen in Luke 10 and across the pages of scripture, these families form and the good news of the Kingdom once again comes as a treasure worth all we have.

However, to see these families formed in our time, we face an odd and often hidden challenge. Around the world, and for most of human history, people have grown up and lived in extended families. Whether in tribal villages, neighborhood clans, or the large, intergenerational household communities of the ancient world, people have lived—for better and for worse—with people they knew well most of their lives. But this is no longer true.

For the past one hundred years or so, humanity has engaged in a vast experiment with a new, more isolated approach to life. With the coming of the automobile and other technologies, we have developed a new "normal" that means we work, play, fight, learn and do business mostly with people we barely know or do not know at all. This far into the experiment, we are beginning to see how this kind of living plays out—what we gain and what we lose by it.

Some of the big losses for us, several generations into this experiment, are the relational values, skills and understanding that support close community. In calling people into vibrant families of Jesus and equipping them for this life, we have found that giving deep attention to these five values is a powerful means to re-discover the life Jesus modeled and called us to live.

We believe the first of our core values, Joy Fueled, is key to the formation of these spiritual families and vital to raising up the kind of leaders who foster them. In this book, we will share what we have learned so far in becoming joy-fueled ourselves and empowering others to join this worldwide, joy-fueled revolution of community.

1

A Journey of Joy

Join Us

Jesus:

"Are you tired? Worn out? Burned out on religion? Come to me. Get away with me and you'll recover your life. I'll show you how to take a real rest. Walk with me and work with me—watch how I do it. Learn the unforced rhythms of grace. I won't lay anything heavy or ill-fitting on you. Keep company with me and you'll learn to live freely and lightly."

Matthew 11:28-30 MSG

RESEARCH SHOWS THAT 65 MILLION AMERICANS are done with church as most know it, but at least half of them are not done with God. Many of these are seasoned pastors, missionaries, church planters, elders, seminary professors or church staff members—in a word: leaders. This mass exodus is a staggering reality that cannot be ignored by those who know and love Jesus. One in every three adults in the United States committed their life to God but has since given up hope of finding joyful community within the churches they have known.

Yet ironically, vibrancy and joy are what we have been promised. Jesus said, "I have come so that they (my sheep) can have real life and eternal life, more and better life than they ever dreamed of" (John 10:10 MSG). And again, "I have told you these

1

things for a purpose: that my joy may be your joy and your joy wholly mature" (John 15:11 MSG).

Sadly, the experience of many who have shared in the life of a congregation and served the church for decades has been the opposite: a guilt-ridden, duty-based, judgmental experience, void of true joy, that has left them still searching for the life Jesus promises.

Perhaps you are one of those people. Perhaps you left the church discouraged, hurt, frustrated, angry, or just apathetic. Maybe you are still there, still trying to effect sustainable transformation but find yourself discouraged and tired, overwhelmed, losing hope.

Either way, you're looking for better answers. You're done being guilted, cajoled, judged and expected upon. You are ready to encounter this joy and vibrant life Jesus has promised is your birthright as a child of God.

We would like to offer you just that: joy as your primary source of motivation that leads to the vibrant life in community that Jesus promised. With our combined 100+ years of Christian ministry in the pastorate, the mission field, church planting and Christian education, John, Kent and I (Toni) have experienced how powerful this joy is and how you can nurture it in yourself, in your family and yes, even in your church—whatever form that might take. Joy, in fact, is a far superior fuel for motivating us to grow and mature emotionally and spiritually.

In the following pages, we will define this joy and explain a common but harmful fuel source or motivation that many of us in the Christian world have succumbed to. Understanding this damaging motivation is so important that we will devote three chapters to it.

In subsequent chapters, we will explore how mission can be a spontaneous explosion of joy. Then we will unpack this motivation from both a scriptural perspective as well as from a neurobiological perspective. Finally, we will reveal the implications of being joy-fueled for individuals as well as all expressions of the church, both locally and globally.

We will also introduce two of our favorite people: Roland Allen, an Anglican priest who wrote almost a hundred years ago about the importance of joy as our primary source of motivation, and Dr. Jim Wilder of Life Model Works, whose study of joy as our primary source of motivation has paved the way for many to find relational wholeness.

Notice we say "primary" source of motivation. We acknowledge that throughout Scripture, other motivations are drawn upon to "spur us on toward love and good deeds" (Hebrew 10:24 NIV), motivations such as fear of bad things happening and pleasure of rewards that could come. We do not want to negate these motivations, as they may all serve good, necessary and helpful roles to a certain point in our human development. However, while they might be useful fuel for a little while, the energy they give dies out.

In *Joy Fueled*, you will discover the only fuel that will go the long haul, lead you into mature relationships with others and with God, and give you the strength to endure the cross set before you. It is the very motivation that allowed Jesus to do the same: joy. "For the joy set before Him He endured the cross" (Hebrews 12:2 NIV).

After 10 years of coaching individuals, families and churches in the joy-fueled way described in these pages, LK10 has seen a spontaneous, world-wide movement spring up. People come to us every day for training and equipping in how to become more vibrant and effectively pass on what they have found. From six continents and across the divides of race, class, culture, privilege and politics, we are seeing joyful community rising. It has been our deep delight to witness this movement emerging. It is our deep joy to share what we are learning.

Now, we offer these experiences, ideas and practices to you. We are confident that Jesus wants to fill you with great delight. There is hope for you to find this vibrancy that comes from joy-fueled relationships. The unforced rhythms of grace we share in these pages not only help you nurture joy in your own life and family but also in the communities you serve. Our online resources document stories from around the world of individuals, families and church leaders like you finding deep delight in connecting heart-to-heart with their loved ones and with the God who loves us.

Do you have all the joy you want?

Would you like to know how to nurture joy in yourself, your family and your community?

Are you ready to reimagine church and reclaim joy as your motivation?

The journey awaits you; the promise is real and we are here to cheer you on.

2

Joy

A Brief Introduction

CLOSE YOUR EYES AND PICTURE the three people closest to you in your life, those you spend most of your time with, or those who mean the most to you.

What do you see?

No, really. Close your eyes for just a minute and draw to mind the three or four intimate relationships you have. Stay there for a minute and notice how these people appear to you.

What do their faces look like? Are they laughing *at* you? Disgusted by you? Ashamed of you? Disappointed in you? Angry at you? Maybe they are not looking at you at all. Maybe they are not noticing you are even there. Or perhaps they are smiling at you? Laughing with you? Enjoying you? Delighting in who you are?

If you can picture someone enjoying you at some point in your life and can imagine their face being glad to be with you, you have just experienced joy.

Perhaps the most revolutionary idea we have come to embrace is that joy is primarily relational. This could be a relationship with God, with another human, or even with yourself! It can also be experienced in memories of joyful moments together, in gift exchanging and acts of service. However, it is primarily experienced when someone enjoys us, delights in who we are and wants to be with us no matter what we are feeling in the moment. We are precious to them and they show it on their face or through their actions.

Joy flows from giving and receiving love—the life of God. God is love, and where love is being expressed and received, the joy of God is also flowing. Nothing brings us closer to the center of all creative power than the joy of God. Sure enough, as scripture says, "The joy of the Lord is your strength" (Nehemiah 8:10 NIV).

In a simple way, we experience this joy whenever we find ourselves in the presence of someone who makes it clear they are glad to be with us no matter what. Maybe it is the sparkle in their eyes when they look at us or a gentle touch when we are sad. The gift of their expressed love draws out our joy.

We now know through studies in neuro-science that this pattern of love-sparking-joy forms the basis from earliest infancy for all healthy human development. When we witness a baby light up in the presence of her smiling mother, we're witnessing the genesis of joy-fuel being formed in another life. This is love embodied—God's life.

The Greek language of the New Testament offers intriguing insight. The words for joy, gift and gratitude are closely related. All share the same root, *char*—pronounced "car." Here's the connection:

Joy —*Chara (delight)*

Gift or Grace—*Charis* (that which brings joy or delight)

Gratitude—*Eucharistia* (joy or delight returned)

These three ideas together, in any language, give us a way to describe what love-in-action looks like. Lovers give a gift to show their delight in the one they love. On receiving the gift, joy wells up in the beloved. Naturally, they say "thank you!" and deeper joy flows back to the lover.

We sometimes say, "Love grows in the dance of joy between gift and gratitude." More love, more joy. When you stop to think about it, this is astounding. What other process do we know that, all by itself, produces more than it starts with? Love-ignited joy is the one perpetual-motion fuel. Nothing else compares.

This feeling of joy that flows from giving and receiving delight taps into God's own life—the most enduring, powerful and motivational fuel of all (ref. John 15:11). Instead of living out of fear of shame, guilt or duty, when we receive from one another and God at the heart level, we experience a deep sense of joy that makes the relationship greater than any problems we face. No doubt, this is what Jesus had in mind when he said, "I have told you this so that my joy may be in you and that your joy may be complete" (John 15:11 NIV).

Two stunning truths to notice here. First, Jesus desires that the very joy and delight in his heart would be in our hearts, that we would feel what he feels. But he doesn't stop there. The second stunning truth is that he wants the joy in our hearts to be full to overflowing. (A better translation than "complete.") If joy is a fuel source, Jesus is saying that he wants our "tank" to be filled beyond full. What a picture of abundance!

When we share this LK10 Core Value, almost everyone says, "Well, of course! Who wouldn't want joy to be their primary motivation for life and ministry?" What is easily missed, however, is how revolutionary this value actually is within the current Christian culture.

We will say more about how we see joy as our primary fuel in later chapters.

For now, let's turn to the limited and ultimately harmful fuel source that many of us have used at some point in our lives: the gospel of knowledge and duty. This motivating source competes with joy, eventually smothering it out altogether. While appearing very spiritual, over time it will not only thwart intended character development but will erode the very lives it flows through.

3

Guilt or Joy?

The Gospel of Knowledge and Duty

SOME YEARS AGO, at a large conference, a speaker shared lots of information about unreached people groups around the world— the billions who do not yet know Christ. He reminded everyone of the Great Commission in Matthew 28. (Most of us have been reminded of the Great Commission dozens of times before.)

Then the speaker began snapping his fingers as if counting time. Tears filled his eyes as he implored the audience:

"Every second, thousands of people are dying without knowing Christ."

Snap. Snap. Snap.

"What are you going to do about it?"

Snap. Snap. Snap.

The large room fell silent as he continued to snap. Many in the audience were crying. They appeared deeply moved and ready to sign up for the tremendous task of reaching their generation for Christ, no matter the cost.

Perhaps you have heard sermons like that or attended conferences with this kind of presentation: *6,500 unreached people groups... 2.5 billion people never heard the name of Jesus... our evangelism and church planting aren't working.... we are debtors to Christ… no amount of sacrifice will compare to what he has done.*

Who could fail to be moved by this presentation? This kind of motivation? We call this the "gospel of knowledge and duty." The more knowledge we have, the more we will feel obliged to serving, and therefore, the more we will serve.

Yet we have several questions.

1. Is this approach effective in the long run? Thousands or even millions of people have been motivated to ministry by this type of presentation. But, is it really good "fuel"?

2. Is this approach healthy? Does it result in emotionally healthy Christians?

3. Is it biblical? Is this the kind of motivation that we see in the Bible?

Effective Fuel? Healthy Fuel? Biblical Fuel?

As we have said, the gospel of knowledge and duty can sound very spiritual, but we contend that these are actually inadequate types of fuel. When knowledge and duty are all we have, they are not really good news (the meaning of *gospel*) because, as Galatians 3:21-22 tells us, in the long run, this knowledge and duty cannot produce righteousness. Only a relationship with Jesus can do that. Knowledge and duty produce guilt and obligation, which can be effective at starting an engine but, unfortunately, this fuel, so to speak, corrodes over time.

These motivations do produce activity. However, there is a terrible price to pay when a person does not mature beyond these motivations into others more sustainable. The results are Christians who are not only exhausted, burned out and disillusioned but also thwarted in their emotional maturity and relational knowledge of God.

Leaders are drawn into ministry for many reasons. Often a dramatic presentation of the great spiritual need in the world and our obligation or duty based on the Great Commission plays a significant part. Again, this conviction is not a bad thing. However, if guilt and obligation continue to be the main motivations, the results are not good. These things do not teach us what to do with our heavy emotions that come with life and ministry—emotions like grief, anger, discouragement, hopelessness and despair. Guilt and duty are not capable of helping us through these difficult times.

The shocking statistics below from one survey: (https://www.soulshepherding.org/pastors-under-stress/) illustrate the long term results in the lives of pastors facing high levels of stress without an adequate joy base.

- 75% of pastors report being "extremely stressed" or "highly stressed"

- 90% feel fatigued and worn out every week

- 80% will not be in ministry 10 years later

- 91% have experienced some form of burnout in ministry

- Seminary-trained pastors average only five years in church ministry

Even more grievous than these results are the destructive behaviors that come as a result of ministering with these ineffectual motivations. In our combined years of ministry alone, we have seen numerous pastors and/or their spouses end up in inappropriate sexual relationships or substance abuse in an attempt to numb the destructive feelings they do not know how to handle. Many lives, marriages and whole communities are destroyed when this happens. We are convinced that these statistics and experiences would be different if the people of God understood the danger of living guilt-based or duty-driven compared to the amazing power of living joy-fueled.

The story for missionaries is similar. They often answer the call into ministry when, in a sermon or at a conference, the world's great spiritual need is presented. No doubt, in addition to guilt, they feel the Spirit move them as well. However, without emotionally maturing into joy as a sustainable fuel source, the "rest of the story" is told in the attrition statistics that say 71% of missionaries quit serving overseas before their assignment is finished. A 1995 study analyzed the 5,000 missionaries who were quitting every year. In the final analysis, 453 mission agencies from 14 different countries came to find that the main preventable reason missionaries were leaving their field of service was because they needed clearer direction from God to go. In other words, they had gone to serve overseas when mission work was clearly not for them. The other two top reasons for attrition were lack of training and emotional care needed to stay engaged in their field of service.

Here's how missionary kid, Christian psychologist and author, Dr. Jim Wilder, described his experience. (Note: We are indebted to Life Model Works and especially Dr. Jim Wilder for much of what we have learned about being joy-fueled.)

One morning as I read Paul's admonition in Galatians 6:9, "Let us not become weary in doing good," I thought to myself: *That is easy for you to say! I already feel tired and it isn't even afternoon.* I might have added that my work was not as draining as dealing with the workers with whom I shared the tasks. Perhaps you can relate.

Hard work and anxiety were wearing me out, but most of it was self-generated... I was also struggling with a sense of anxiety that was burning up all my excess energy and robbing me of rest.

Discovering and using the highest-grade motivation available not only helped me recover quickly from the weariness that would set in, it helped me guide others to keep a rewarding pace that allowed them to add their creativity and energy to our mission. I have seen the crushing lifestyle that I once lived get the better of some of the most powerful leaders I have known. In fact, far too many leaders and groups who follow them are drawing their motivation from the wrong power source. As a result, they are running on fumes and wondering how much longer they can go on.

(Warner and Wilder, *RARE Leadership*, pp. 33-34)

We relate to Dr. Wilder's experience all too well. All three of us (John, Toni, Kent) have experienced the exact same story personally and with those we have trained and pastorally cared for over the years.

Unforced Rhythms of Grace

Jesus says it this way in Matthew 11:28-29 MSG:

Are you tired? Worn out? Burned out on religion? Come to me. Get away with me and you'll recover your life. I'll show you how to take a real rest. Walk with me and work with me—watch how I do it. Learn the unforced rhythms of grace. I won't lay anything heavy or ill-fitting on you. Keep company with me and you'll learn to live freely and lightly.

In the LK10 Community, we are committed to helping people learn the unforced rhythms of grace by walking and working with Jesus. The word *unforced* is particularly important. We think this is what it means to be joy fueled. Instead of forcing ourselves to do and be, we show our weakness, our exhaustion, our true feelings and we let Jesus meet us there, hold us, invite us into his joy and pull us through. We think this is a radical departure from the ways that Christians have often been motivated in the past, just as it was a radical departure for the Jewish leaders when Jesus said it 2,000 years ago.

If you are anything like us, you may be wondering: *With such a beautiful invitation from Jesus himself to work from a rested, joy-filled space, why do we not enter into it more often and let it motivate us?*

Good question. It reminds us of when God said to the Hebrews: "In repentance and rest is your salvation, in quietness and trust is your strength, but you would have none of it!" (Isaiah 30:15 NIV).

Apparently, it is very difficult for us to rest and receive strength. We seem to gravitate towards trying to prove ourselves worthy. In order to better grasp why we, as God's people, avoid entering into His rest, we need to understand more about the two parts of this inferior motivation: knowledge and duty.

4

Inferior Fuel

Knowledge and Duty

DO YOU KNOW WHAT HAPPENS IN SEMINARY? This is the context in which all three of us were trained. It's where many Christian leaders are trained. Seminary students have classes on church history, systematic theology, hermeneutics (interpreting Scripture), homiletics (how to preach and motivate with more information), and many other subjects. They listen to lectures, read books, write papers, take tests. All of this is focused on gaining more knowledge. The general assumption is that learning more is key to maturity, motivation and transformation (changed lives). But is this really true? Does knowing more by itself produce sustainable motivation?

Some years ago, John was mentoring a seminary student. Towards the end of his time in seminary, this young man reflected on his experience. "Seminary has primarily taught me to be analytical and critical. We analyze everything. Passages of Scripture, sermons, church government, etc. However, what I realize is that when I entered seminary, I was like a grape. I'm leaving as a raisin. I'm all dried up spiritually."

Here is Toni's experience in this regard.

Toni:

By the time I got to seminary (in the '90s), it was more hands-on than most seminaries. The professors had seen

15

that knowledge alone was not the key to transformation, so they tried to make it practical and experiential. There was a focus on trying to help us live what we were learning. However, they still functioned with the premise that if we understood right/true concepts intellectually about God, then we would eventually connect with God in a powerful way. Unfortunately for many, this was not the case.

Sadly, there was also no instruction on connecting with our own hearts, much less the hearts of others. Nor did they train us in how to sense God's voice or presence apart from intellectually studying the Bible. Sensing God speaking to you was a mystery that everyone had to figure out for themselves. But the reality was that most of us were just fumbling in the dark without any experiential sense of God's leadership or presence.

Occasionally someone would sense God's direction in a tangible way, but those moments were rare. In fact, some professors even believed that God only spoke through the Scriptures. So, we were amiss to expect a live, interactive relationship with God in our hearts, our imaginations or in nature like David models in the Psalms. We had to settle for listening to God through reading the Bible alone. But that same Bible pointed to a much more dynamic knowing of God through many means—internal urging, vision, nature and community. This God seems to have an unlimited communication palate, fully customized to the people and situation at hand.

Does Knowledge Produce Godly Character?

Although knowledge and information are absolutely essential, and we are deeply thankful for all of the good teaching we have had, in our experience, these alone are inadequate when it comes to producing maturity, motivation and transformation. If they were truly effective for character change, seminary graduates would uniformly be the most emotionally mature, godly people around. And America, where there is no end to knowledge through sermons, seminars, books and podcasts, would be by far the godliest nation on earth.

This obsession with seeking knowledge is particularly noticeable in the proliferation of conferences and retreats characterized by the "sage on the stage" syndrome. We leave these events with pages of notes—some of us have shelves filled with notebooks from all of the conferences, seminars and classes we have attended—but life change is often minimal. The sad fact is that surveys consistently show that the typical Christian in the U.S. looks pretty much like any other person in terms of basic life choices. Misguided notions of knowledge have left American Christians overfed and undernourished and woefully ineffective.

But Jesus said, "You will know the truth and the truth will set you free" (John 8:32 NIV). Isn't knowing the truth important?

Yes, of course, truth is important. But the way this scripture is often quoted implies the opposite of what Jesus was really saying. Here's how we paraphrase the whole text:

> To the Jews who believed in him, Jesus said, "If you make my word the place you actually live, you are my disciples in fact, and you will know the truth, and the truth will set you free."

17

The Jews following Jesus already knew scripture well, and at some level they were believing his claims. Yet he was looking for something more in his followers—the kind of knowledge produced by living experience with him—the living Word.

What exactly did Jesus mean by *truth*? He gives us the answer when He says, "I am the way, the truth, and the life." This means that truth is actually a person, Jesus himself, not merely a collection of information.

Jim Wilder and Marcus Warner help us understand which kind of truth transforms lives and which does not. Their book, *The Solution of Choice: Four Good Ideas that Neutralized Western Christianity,* shares four ideas that seemed good at the time but have actually taken the power out of our faith. One of these dangerous "good ideas that neutralized Western Christianity" is that left-brain, propositional truth will produce godly character and sustainable transformation. Here's the way they say it:

"Since the days of the enlightenment, we have lived in an increasingly left-brain dominated world of virtual reality, redundant information, and relational isolation. Sadly, the church has simply followed along, unable to see what we have lost in our abandonment of all God intended the right brain to do. Therefore, we have a problem-focused, analytical church that is good at doing tasks and talking about ideas. What we have missed is a church that excels at empathy, compassion, forming deep bonds, and loving our enemies" (p. 31).

Wilder and Warner go on to explain that Western Christianity has overemphasized propositional truth (left-brain) and underemphasized relational truth (right-brain). Relational truth is reflected in the Hebrew word *yada* which is translated "to know." It is not enough to know *about* God. He wants us to know him in a deep, communal, experiential way. And... he wants us to let him know us in the same way.

Jesus addressed this problem with the Jews.

> *You have your heads in your Bibles constantly because you think you'll find eternal life there. But you miss the forest for the trees. These Scriptures are all about me! And here I am, standing right before you, and you aren't willing to receive from me the life you say you want.*

John 5:39-40 MSG

These Jews were the smartest and best scripturally-educated people around. No one knew the Scriptures better than they did. But what they totally missed was exactly what those very Scriptures pointed toward—a relationship with Jesus.

We affirm that both ways of knowing are important. It's not head or heart, but head *and* heart. We in LK10 are seeking to restore a balance by equipping and training people in how to connect with each other and with God on a heart level as well as a head level. For example, in our Church 101 course, people learn to practice two simple rhythms of attention as a pathway to relational connection. Pastors, missionaries, elders, seasoned and new Christians alike finally discover a relationship with God that they only dreamed was possible.

Given that knowledge as propositional, left-brain truth alone does not result in godly character or sustainable transformation, it is inadequate to motivate us in ministry and mission.

Did Knowledge Move the Disciples to Mission?

Consider the disciples. Here's the commission that Jesus gave them...

> *All authority in heaven and on earth has been given to me. Therefore go and make disciples of all nations, baptizing them in the name of the Father and of the Son and of the Holy Spirit, and teaching them to obey everything I have commanded you.*

Matthew 28:18-20

The part of this instruction that the disciples couldn't process was "all nations." They had walked with Jesus for three years in Israel. They were all Jews and understood making disciples of other Jews. But that was the limit of their thinking. The Greek word for *nations* is *ethne*, which can also be translated as "gentiles." A gentile is simply someone who isn't a Jew and is therefore a heathen and a pagan. During Jesus' time, many Jews took such pride in their cultural and religious heritage that they considered Gentiles "unclean," calling them "dogs" and "the uncircumcised." To make matters worse, it was the Roman Gentiles who were the hated occupiers of Israel at that time. It's hard for us today to imagine the negative feelings that Jews in Israel, including, no doubt, the disciples, had towards gentiles.

We see this inward focus in Acts 1:6. Jesus had given specific instructions to make disciples of all the nations/gentiles. The disciples don't even ask about that. Rather, the only question they can think about has to do with Israel. "Lord, are you at this time going to restore the kingdom to Israel?"

They simply couldn't imagine anything outside of Israel and the Jewish people. So, Jesus, after refusing to answer their question, once again shows the scope of what he is thinking. He

20

told them that when the Spirit comes on you, you will be my witnesses in Jerusalem ("Ok, we can do that."), and in all Judea and Samaria ("Ok, maybe we can do that."), and to the ends of the earth. ("I'm sorry. What did you say?")

So, what eventually motivated the disciples to go to the ends of the earth and share the good news of Christ with the gentile nations? It wasn't the knowledge of the great need of the world to know Jesus. And, it wasn't even the specific instructions of their master, Jesus. It was only the active presence of the Holy Spirit with them that could bridge the cultural gap and guide them into attempting the seemingly impossible.

Because Jesus knew that neither knowledge nor duty nor hope in his coming presence would be enough for the task at hand, he directed their steps to gather together and wait for his promised presence. The only motivation strong enough to move them across the huge cultural divide to reach gentiles and to sustain this revolution of joy that was about to be unleashed was God's people filled with God's Spirit, overflowing in bold, joyful community to the world around them.

This is why, in LK10 communities, we do not exhort people into missions or house church planting or any other kind of ministry. Rather, we help them develop an intimate, communal and conversational relationship with Jesus, and we trust the Spirit to lead them exactly where he wants them to go. Ministry is the spontaneous, un-exhorted by-product of that beautiful heart-to-heart connection with the living God. It is out of God's deep desire to enjoy us fully that he ignites our hearts for the world. He is not a God who just wants to use us for his benefit. He wants to fill us first and foremost, to restore us to all we were created to be and then lead us into our destiny.

That begs the question, "How do we sense God, let him enjoy us, and let Him lead us?" While we will unfold some practices in these pages, we refer you to LK10's Church 101 course for the opportunity to train in these very skills. For now, however, let's continue exploring the damaging fuel of duty and contrast it with the life-giving fuel of joy.

5

What Fuels You?

Futility of Duty, Obligation and Shame

DURING OUR YEARS OF PASTORAL MINISTRY, teaching at seminary and church planting, like most Christian leaders we struggled with the question of how to motivate the people we were leading. Unfortunately, what was modeled for us and what we used as fuel was all too often a sense of obligation and duty.

Frustrated with people's lack of commitment and engagement, and not knowing a better way to incite the masses to action, we communicated in a steady stream of "shoulds" and "oughts." We would never resort to words like *guilt* or *shame*, but in reality, that's what we were doing to trigger people.

We realized early on that guilt and shame fueled people's base instincts of survival and fear, and so their actions were a reaction to these emotions. Because of this, we could drive the people only so far until they either broke down, quit or just moved on.

This is especially true when using duty and obligation as fuel for motivating people to enter the mission field. This form of the gospel, which uses fear to motivate people to activity, has substantially failed over time at changing lives and making disciples, which is the basis of sustainable transformation. In addition, it has a number of unintended negative consequences that might even need professional care to help heal.

Here's what these pseudo motivations can sound like. Yes, they are based on fact, but are in fact not intended to motivate us but to ground us. Joy is our fuel for motivation.

- We are saved by Jesus' sacrifice.
- We are debtors to Christ.
- We owe Him our very lives.
- No amount of sacrifice compares to what Christ has done.
- Therefore, we must go and do the same.

John Piper calls this the "debtor's ethic" in his book, *Future Grace*. He points out that this way of motivating Christians is quite common in contemporary church culture but is almost entirely absent in Scripture.

There is an impulse in the fallen human heart—in all our hearts—to forget that gratitude is a spontaneous response of joy to receiving something over and above what we paid for. Pay special attention to the word *spontaneous*. When we forget this, gratitude starts to be misused and distorted as an impulse to pay for the very thing that came to us gratis, meaning "free." This terrible moment of forgetting is the birthplace of the debtor's ethic.

The debtor's ethic says, "Because you have done something good for me, I feel *indebted* to do something good for you." This impulse is *not* what gratitude was designed to produce. God meant gratitude to be a spontaneous expression of pleasure in the gift and the goodwill of another. He did not mean it to be an impulse to return favors. If gratitude is twisted into a sense of debt, it gives birth to the debtor's ethic, and the effect is to nullify grace.

Trusting Emotions

Because the gospel of duty tends to focus on tasks above relationships, it also has a tendency to corrode or minimize relationships. Repeatedly, we have heard, "We are responsible for fulfilling the Great Commission. We have important work to do and we had better get busy doing it." This is what Wilder and Warner refer to when they say, "We have a problem-focused, analytical church that is good at doing tasks and talking about ideas." But where is the focus on the relationship with God that Jesus seemed to have? Here is a personal story from John White.

> Some years ago, when I was on staff at a megachurch, the senior pastor met with the pastoral staff one day and said: "I want to caution you about having an expectation that we will be friends. You were all hired to do a job. It is unrealistic to expect that we will also be friends."

> Although I didn't say it out loud at the time, I thought to myself how sad this was, tragic really. The leadership of the church was so focused on "the work of God" that we were not able to model for the congregation what it was to be "the people of God."

> Implicit in the gospel of duty is that emotions are suspect and even dangerous. Consider the mantra of the stalwart Christian soldier: "We must do our duty regardless of how we feel." To reinforce this concept early in my Christian life, the metaphor of a train was explained to me. The locomotive of the train represents the facts of the Christian life—who Jesus is, what he has done for us, etc. The next car after the locomotive is our faith. The caboose at the end represents our feelings or emotions. Here's the message: "The facts drive the train. We put

our faith in those facts and our feelings may or may not come along behind. Focus all of your attention on the facts. Don't be distracted by your feelings."

While that illustration made a lot of sense to me as a young Christian, I've learned since that denying my emotions is both unhealthy and unbiblical. Emotions are a window into our hearts. They are like the indicator lights on the dashboard of our car. However, because many of us have no idea how to handle our emotions, we fear them, bury them, deny them and eventually medicate them so that we can press on with the mission at hand.

The interesting part to all of this is that we have counseling and soul-care departments in our organizations to try to help people who are not successfully managing their emotions. The sad danger in this is that soul care and mission have become separate entities all together within Christendom. Jesus never separated soul care from mission. For him, they were one and the same. We must seek to integrate soul care and mission again, approaching ourselves holistically and letting God have and love all of us. The missional church movement, unfortunately, has propagated some of this mission-driven reality.

The Missional Church Movement

There is another expression of the gospel of duty found in some sectors of the missional church movement. Out of a desire to see the Kingdom of God advance, certain leaders make mission the primary purpose and obligation of the church. That perspective, born out of a desire to motivate God's people, is understandable. Plus, it sounds so...biblical. We believe, however, that while it contributes amazing ideas for how to embed into a society and share the gospel with the world around us, it misses the actual biblical source of motivation in the process. Unintentionally, this movement has used language that has shifted the focus from the King to the Kingdom.

Mike Breen, one of the leaders of that movement, came to this conclusion. Here are some key quotes from his blog:

It's time we start being brutally honest about the missional movement that has emerged in the last 10-15 years: Chances are better than not it's going to fail.

That may seem cynical, but I'm being realistic. There is a reason so many movements in the Western church have failed in the past century: They are a car without an engine. A missional church or a missional community or a missional small group is the new car that everyone is talking about right now, but no matter how beautiful or shiny the vehicle, without an engine, it won't go anywhere.

We are a group of people addicted to and obsessed with the work of the Kingdom, with little to no idea how to be with the King.

Many church leaders unknowingly replace the transcendent vitality of a life with God for the ego satisfaction they derive from a life for God.

Toni's experience reveals the complexity of the missional focus. While incredibly good things seem to be achieved through being missional, there is a terrible cost on the leaders who confuse the success of the mission with their closeness to Christ.

Toni:

I can attest to this reality. For many years as a church planter in Uruguay, my husband, Matt, and I began a few missional movements and missional communities, each successful and very attractive to both the secular world and the Christian world around us. Christians were challenged, not-yet-believers came to know Jesus, and many leaders in Uruguay were amazed and inspired by what was possible. I am forever grateful for the results of all the good that was experienced.

With each movement, however, we eventually realized that our young leaders and, honestly ourselves, were burning out instead of maturing and feeling joy-fueled. As it turned out, none of those we were working with (including us) could feel God's deep delight personally with any consistency, nor could we sense God's constant presence loving, attuning and guiding us. Matt and I began a journey to discover why this was. What we found was that being joy-fueled is actually how humans were created to function as a result of emotional maturity. In the church, however, little has been taught on emotional maturity over the years. This deficiency has developed leaders who are lacking in this area.

I understand that the missional movement, as some propose, begins with relationship with Jesus. And the leaders I know personally definitely share from an intimate knowledge of God. However, while I was under the teaching of missional leaders, they never once taught us how to sense God's presence and direction, individually or communally. It seemed that they quickly moved into a different paradigm of knowledge and duty, focusing on how well we can exegete culture and form effective strategies to reach people for Christ.

There was rarely a discussion of mission as an overflow. Rather, it seemed like an expectation that we *should* be on mission because Jesus is on mission.

Overflow is a keyword here. At times, it felt like the missional movement saw mission as our responsibility, duty and obligation. Therefore, we were told we must exhort people to get busy reaching out to neighbors and organizing missional communities because it was our mandate and what true followers of Jesus do.

Overflow

What we have come to believe today, with Roland Allen's help, is that biblical mission is a spontaneous overflow and is, by definition, un-exhorted. When they say that "all Christians should be involved in the Great Commission of Jesus," it sounds good and logical, but anytime there is a *should* in there, it often leads to the gospel of knowledge and duty.

As a result of this focus on mission instead of relational overflow, many mission organizations and churches have needed to form soul-care divisions where missionaries and pastors can find personal support as they approach burnout. Yet what if soul care and mission were not two different pursuits but one and the same? What if soul care was actually the fuel for mission?

We doubt seriously that this guilt-ridden motivation is what the leaders had in mind in the early stages of the missional movement. However, there is a serious lack of integration in Christian leadership that has to be addressed. Self-worth that is derived solely from mission is one of them. Soul care and mission being separated in one's life is another.

Addictions often form to hide pain and give a sense of self-worth (albeit it a false sense). For many Christian leaders (including ourselves) our drug of choice was not alcohol or overeating but accomplishment, achievement, getting stuff done for Jesus and helping others… instead of learning to give and receive from others. Unfortunately, in spite of the positive intentions, the missional movement fits right into these addictions perfectly and fuels them. But this fuel eventually runs out.

Mission cannot be the organizing principle of the church. It must be Jesus—knowing him, sensing him in the present, feeling his joy over us, hearing his voice and following that voice. He will always lead us on mission, yes. However, his timeline is often very different than ours. Sometimes, it doesn't even look like what we think it should.

Sometimes, Jesus leads us on mission to seek and save all that was lost inside of us and our nuclear families. Following him there might be deemed as "inward-focused" by others. Are we willing to go there even if we get no self-worth out of it? Even if it doesn't look hip? Even if it doesn't seem to be bringing lost people into the Kingdom? Even if it is not fundable? Can we trust Jesus' leadership in our lives and in the lives of others to lead them into mission in his way and in his time?

If so, then, what would happen if we focused on helping people mature to a consistent, vibrant relationship with Jesus, with themselves and with those around them? Could that be what "making disciples" is all about? What if we coached them on their connections and let Jesus do the rest to coach them in being "church" and living on "mission" individually and as a community?

While we have no doubt the focus on mission is well-intentioned, we believe it is misguided. In Scripture, mission is not the focus. Think about it. How many times is the Great Commission repeated in the Epistles? None! The church's "organizing principle" was never meant to be a mission.

We see this communicated clearly in Paul's prayers for the churches. His understanding is that if the people of God are filled with the love of God, then the mission of God will overflow spontaneously. His prayers, therefore, focus on the church being filled with God's love and grace. He prays that they would know Christ, that they would learn to receive Jesus more, that they would come to a deeper experience of his love for them and the power of that love so that there will be unity, wholeness, right living, etc.

Here are some examples of his prayers.

May the God of hope fill you with all joy and peace as you trust in him, so that you may overflow with hope by the power of the Holy Spirit.

Romans 15:13 NIV

I keep asking that the God of our Lord Jesus Christ... give you the Spirit of wisdom and revelation, so that you may know him better... that the eyes of your heart may be enlightened.

Ephesians 1:17-18 NIV

I pray...that he may strengthen you with power...in your inner being, so that Christ may dwell in your hearts through faith...that you...may have power,

31

*together with all the Lord's holy people, to grasp...
the love of Christ, and to know this love... that you
may be filled to the measure of all the fullness of
God.*

Ephesians 3:16-19 NIV

*And this is my prayer: that your love may abound
more and more in knowledge and depth of insight,
so that you may be able to discern what is best and
may be pure and blameless for the day of Christ,
filled with the fruit of righteousness that comes
through Jesus Christ—to the glory and praise of
God.*

Philippians 1:9-11 NIV

*May the Lord make your love increase and
overflow for each other and for everyone else, just
as ours does for you.*

1 Thessalonians 3:12 NIV

*I constantly remember you in my prayers. Recalling
your tears, I long to see you, so that I may be filled
with joy.*

2 Timothy 1:3-4 NIV

Multiple times he prays that peace and grace be with them
all (ref. 1 Corinthians 16:23; Galatians 6:18; Philippians 4:23; 1
Thessalonians 5:28; 2 Thessalonians 3:16; 2 Timothy 4:22; Titus
3:15b; Philemon 25).

It seems clear to us that for Paul, the organizing principle of
the church is learning to be with the King—to experience his
grace, to delve into his love, to receive deeply from his resources
and riches. Once we all realized that Jesus was responsible for

building his church and that our responsibility was to let him radically love us, let him speak to us and guide us so we could love him, ourselves and each other, we felt a great weight lift off of our chests. We were free to learn to receive and give, not just give until we were burned out and empty.

It now makes sense that if people are not spontaneously giving and sharing, it is because they are not full and overflowing. When we begin to focus, as Paul did, on helping people learn to connect with God and others heart-to-heart in a powerful way, it fuels them with joy to overflowing.

What surprises us even more is that the one time Paul does pray that the church would be active in sharing their faith, the motivation he gives them is far from guilt. He does not share the lostness of the world or the needs at hand but rather motivates them by saying that if they share their faith, they will actually experience Christ even more! He says in Philemon:

> *I pray that you may be active in sharing your faith*
> *so that you will have a full understanding of every*
> *good thing we have in Christ. Your love has given*
> *me great joy and encouragement.*

Philemon 6-7 NIV

To bring this home, look at the passion of Jesus' prayer for his bride in John 17, just before his crucifixion. He does not pray that they will plant churches, understand the strategy or figure out how to get the gospel out into the world. Instead, he prays for a deeper sense of identity, knowing that if they know by experience who they are and whose they are, somehow the world will know he sent them. He prays for protection so that they can live as one (v. 11-12). He says these things while he is with them "so that they may have the full measure" of His joy within them (v. 13). He again

33

prays for their protection and oneness because he believes that when they are brought into complete unity, "I in them and you [God] in me—so that they may be brought to complete unity. Then the world will know that you sent me and have loved them even as you have loved me" (v. 23).

Everything Jesus did was because he intimately knew the Father. We will talk more on this in the next section. However, it is relevant here to say that joy was Christ's motivation for going to the cross. Joy, the knowledge that God was glad to be with him no matter what, and that he would one day be with all of us, motivated Jesus to sacrifice his life willingly. It was an overflow of delight, not the obligation of mission. The lack of sacrifice in ourselves and the church today is a direct result of a lack of this type of joy.

The church's focus, its organizing principle, is meant to be an intimate, conversational, communal, love relationship with Jesus and each other. Mission flows out of these joy-filled relationships. A significant biblical metaphor is the bride (i.e. the church) who is passionate about her bridegroom (ref. Ephesians 5:25-27; Revelation 19:7-9). Mission is the spontaneous by-product of that relationship.

> *Righteous Father, though the world does not know you, I know you, and they know that you have sent me. I have made you known to them and will continue to make you known in order that the love you have for me may be in them and that I myself may be in them.*
>
> John 17:25-26 NIV

6

Joy Fuel

Mission as An Explosion of Joy

WITHIN ALL OF OUR WORKING TEAMS within LK10's leadership, being joy-fueled is non-negotiable. In every single meeting, the Oversight Team, the Research and Development Team, and the Communications Team each take time to share appreciation stories with each other as well as to share how we are currently feeling. Some days, when emotions are heavier, that leaves us little time to work or strategize as we take time to listen to Jesus together about tough issues. Because connecting heart-to-heart like this takes time, occasionally we have wondered how in the world we get anything done at all!

Why do we do this? Because we have become convinced that joy is a top-grade fuel, a source of motivation that is superior in every way.

The amazing thing is that a lot gets done because maturity happens and energy is released when we feel seen, heard and loved by each other and by God. Also, there is little conflict between us because we are so glad to be together even when we disagree. Therefore, conflict does not drain our energy but is a welcome ally. We seek to deeply respect each other's opinions and we listen to Jesus together about everything. He always gives us insight and creates a path forward.

Out of this joy, a global training organization has birthed itself over the last 12 years. It has grown from a handful of people practicing loving each other and listening to God, to hundreds of people in over 23 different countries and 6 different languages (at the writing of this book). We do not advertise or try to get people to join us for training. Rather, we love God and each other well, and we pray that God will send people to us to train to do the same. They have spontaneously come, hundreds of them: pastors, missionaries, lawyers, parents, businessmen and women and young adults (to name a few).

Toni and Matt's experience with the missional movement reminds us of what Roland Allen wrote in *The Spontaneous Expansion of the Church* in 1927. No one, in our opinion, expresses the idea of joy as motivation or fuel for the Christian life and ministry more clearly than he does. The opening paragraphs of his book (see quote below) are as devastating to today's prevailing Christian culture as they were to the culture of Allen's day. What he saw was that the church had significantly departed from the biblical perspective on missions.

> When we turn from the restless entreaties and exhortations which fill the pages of our modern missionary magazines to the pages of the New Testament, we are astonished at the change in the atmosphere. St. Paul does not repeatedly exhort his churches to subscribe money for the propagation of the faith. Instead, he is far more concerned to explain to them what the faith is and how they ought to practice it and keep it.

> The same is true of St. Peter and St. John and of all the apostolic writers. They do not seem to feel any necessity to repeat the great Commission and to urge that it is the duty of their converts to make disciples of all the nations. What we read in the New Testament is no anxious appeal

to Christians to spread the Gospel, but a note here and there which suggests how the Gospel was being spread abroad.

For centuries the Christian Church continued to expand by its own inherent grace and threw up an unceasing supply of missionaries without any direct exhortation" (p. 7).

As we established in the previous chapter, missions in the New Testament occurred "without any direct exhortation." Hubert Allen explains in his book, *Roland Allen: Pioneer, Priest, and Prophet*, that motivation for mission came from the Holy Spirit. He alone is the "active agent in Christian mission." When we truly believe that, we are "delivered from the anxieties, the burdens and the sense of guilt which so often come from the atmosphere of discussion about mission." Mission should never be conceived of as a task, rather "as a gift, an over-spill, and an explosion of joy" (1998, p xiii).

In other words, for Roland Allen, mission is joy-fueled.

We also see John Piper writing about this spontaneous affection as motivation for worship in *Desiring God: Meditations of a Christian Hedonist*. "Worship," Piper claims, "cannot be done by mere acts of duty. It can only be done when spontaneous affections arise in the heart."

We argue that "spontaneous affections" only arise in the heart when we learn to receive from the God who loves us when we let him enjoy us. So much of the Christian life seems to be about doing for God: worshiping him, serving him, suffering for him, etc. Yet we have forgotten that all of this is birthed out of letting him know us inside and out, letting him see our hearts and letting him love the lovable and unlovable within us. It is then that spontaneous affections arise. When we move into Christian life and service without feeling God's deep love and enjoyment of us, our service becomes nothing more than good works to make us feel better about ourselves.

As Piper laments later in that same book: "The sad thing about ALL of this is that when duty is the focus, we make ourselves the center and cut ourselves off from the source."

We could not have said it better.

Spontaneous

As *spontaneous* has come up with both John Piper and Roland Allen, it's important to stop and take note. First, let us define the word.

Spontaneous: from *sponte* meaning voluntarily, occurring without apparent external cause, unconstrained and unstudied in behavior (Merriam-Webster dictionary).

John:

I have come to love this word *spontaneous*. It first caught my attention when I heard the title of the book by Roland Allen that we mentioned previously, *The Spontaneous Expansion of the Church and the Causes that Hinder It*. It was several years before I actually read the book but something about the title stayed with me.

I wondered how the expansion of the church could be spontaneous. This was so different from what I had been taught and experienced in church. I had become a follower of Jesus at the age of 15. And, for the next 12 years, through high school, college and seminary, I was involved in a ministry that was characterized by the phrase "make it happen." That is, Scripture gave us our marching orders and it was our job to get busy, do ministry and build the church. In some ways, this ministry was quite successful and resulted in huge youth groups. However, there wasn't much about it that was spontaneous.

This mentality was reinforced in Fuller Seminary in 1973 when I found myself in one of the first classes on "church growth theory" taught in the United States. Church growth was our job. By working hard and applying certain principles, we could see the church grow. There was nothing spontaneous about this either.

For the next 25 years, as a pastor in several churches, I worked hard at applying those principles as a youth pastor, small groups pastor, adult ministries pastor and church planting pastor.

The "make it happen" approach applied not only to the church and ministry but also to my own Christian life. It was my job to get busy and work hard at loving God and growing as a Christian. I did this by having a quiet time first thing every morning. I actively pursued inductive Bible study, meditation on the Word, and prayer (which was a monologue, of course). I worked hard at being faithful to attend church and Bible study, to pray for and witness to my friends, and to love my wife and children.

At the same time, I was also working hard at ignoring my emotions. Emotions were dangerous and distracting and unreliable.

Such was the Christian life for me and for most everyone I knew. The only problem was that all of this was exhausting. Spontaneous affection towards God, my wife, my family and friends was not something I paid attention to. Plus, if I had to stuff my fear, hurt, shame and anger, that meant stuffing appreciation and joy as well. I was taught that the Christian life was to be lived by my will. So, that's what I tried to do. I was living out the gospel of knowledge and duty.

There was no room to feel at all.

Gospel of Joy

The alternative to the gospel of knowledge and duty that we are proposing is a gospel of joy, where we sense God being glad to be with us no matter what we are feeling. Jet fuel. Where we feel Him with us in these emotions, listening, empathizing and gently encouraging, healing and correcting. Living in this kind of intimate, conversational relationship with the Holy Spirit and others results in an organic and spontaneous overflow in one's Christian life and ministry.

> *The world cannot accept him [the Spirit - Paraklete in Greek], because it neither sees him nor knows him. But you know him, for he lives with you and will be in you.*

John 14:17 NIV (emphasis added)

With that kind of promise and power, let's step back and look at the source of our joy.

7

The Ultimate Fuel

What Kind of God?

DUTY-DRIVEN, JOYLESS RELIGION IS THE PERFECT LIE—miserable bad news posing as the life of God and demanding that this be our life too. But who is God, really, and what is the life of God actually like?

In early July this year, Toni's husband, Matt, told us a story we can't stop thinking about. Matt had asked his nine-year-old son Matty, "What would you like to do today, buddy?" The boy had just seen a picture of his sister with a praying mantis she had discovered on a camping trip. Feeling not-so-special and a little jealous, Matty replied, "I'd like to see a praying mantis."

"Ok," Dad said, "Let's ask God." They prayed out loud, "Lord, let us see a praying mantis." Then they went for a five-mile bike ride, stopping every so often to look for a mantis on the plants around them. They didn't find one. Tired and disappointed, Matt said nothing more about the unanswered prayer to his son.

That evening, the Daniels family was hosting some visiting friends for dinner on their back patio. Matt prayed for the meal. When the "amen" was said, a baby, half-inch praying mantis was sitting on little Matty's table knife. The boy's squeal of delight filled the air and all were amazed! Just as requested, a mantis showed up right in time for prayer—a *praying* mantis!

When we tell that story, people laugh and are delighted with amazement. We promise them: it's true. We have the video to prove it. But the story doesn't end there.

Kent:

I loved the story so much that I shared it with a group of LK10 leaders on a video conference. By the end of that call, I had been sitting for three hours, so I stepped outside to stretch and check the weather. There on the hedge by our front gate was—I kid you not—a tiny praying mantis. It was the first one I had seen in over a year. And yes, I have the video to prove it.

I want to pause here and invite you to a deeper observation. This story is so amusing, even cute, that it would be easy to miss its importance. What sort of God is this who is aware of the hope of a nine-year-old and his dad on a summer day in Nashville, Tennessee? What kind of God is so interested, caring and powerful to arrange the arrival of the requested gift at that particular moment on that particular knife?

And, to provide a second witness that this story was no accident, what God would arrange for a second mantis of the same size to arrive on a particular hedge in Abilene, Texas at the exact moment it would be seen by the man who had just shared the story?

Two weeks later, our family was out one evening in the Texas countryside with a few families exploring the night sky through a telescope. That's when the significance of the mantis story hit me at a whole new level. I was reminded of the size of Earth in relation to the other heavenly bodies we were observing: Jupiter with its shining moons, 1300 times the volume of Earth; our local star, the Sun, just below the horizon, amazing that 1,200,000 Earths would fit in that glowing, burning ball.

We could see our Milky Way Galaxy strung across the night sky, made up of two hundred billion stars. And our galaxy as just one of what we're now being told are two trillion galaxies, give or take a few.

Two trillion galaxies. A mantis on a table knife. The contrast left me stunned, almost breathless. It stuns me still. Incomprehensible power coupled with infinitely tender, intimate care. Holy Love.

The Hebrew word we usually translate as "glory" in English carries two major ideas. On the one hand, it means heavy, weighty, substantial. On the other hand, it conveys the idea of brilliant, shining, radiant. In the physical realm, a star is literally glorious—stunningly massive and radiant at the same time.

The kind of God we are dealing with is called in scripture the Glorious One. This God is substantial to the degree that, with a word he calls the universe into being. This God is radiant to the degree that he relentlessly gives himself away with creative, playful joy.

This joy is a fuel that never runs out.

8

In The Beginning

An Invitation Into Delight

WHERE DOES JOY COME FROM? How is it perpetuated? Ultimately, this fuel comes straight from the dance of giving and receiving within the shared life of God—the Father, Son and Spirit. Joy is the story of God's own self, foundational to all other stories, the master story of stories.

This is our story, as told by Kent. Having taught university students with short attention spans for many years, he has learned to tell the whole story of history in under 25 seconds. Ready? Here it is:

Kent:

In the beginning was Joy.

In the end will be deeper Joy.

And in between is an astounding invitation: "Come, share in *our* joy."

The story begins even before God says, "Let *us* make people in *our* image."

Even before God makes a place called, "Garden of delight and joy," or *Eden* in the Hebrew language.

Even before God speaks, saying, "Let there be," and "It is very good."

45

Even before the Spirit hovers over the chaos.

Before all of this, there was an amazing communion, a gift-giving community, an interdependent family of love that is Father, Son and Spirit, sharing life in an eternally overflowing dance of joy.

As we fast forward through the pages of scripture, past the fall, past the time when God comes to a man and says "I will bless all the people through you, through your seed," fast forward past when God is with us through Immanuel, Jesus, and shows his compassion toward us, that he loves the whole world so much that he gives his son to demonstrate his relentless love for us.

And if we fast forward all the way through the communities that Jesus initiates, communities that are all about the spontaneous reconciliation of all people to God, we get all the way down to the last pages and verses of Scripture and we see what the point of the story is.

To start with, we find who we would expect. The Father is there on a throne, and the Son is with the Father. The Holy Spirit is there as well, offering an invitation. But another person is present.

This person is key to the deeper joy that marks the end of this story, for she is a beautiful bride who has come to join the eternal celebration of the Family of God. Along with the Spirit, the bride says, "Come." And as you likely know, she is a bride made up of all the families and peoples of the world—all that bear the divine DNA originally imparted to that first family in the garden of delight.

Just to be clear, that includes your people and mine.

Love of the Bride

One way to see the value God places on this bride is to notice what God has been willing to give for her from the moment the story opens, all the way to the end. Gifts, as we have been noticing, are the currency of love, intended to evoke joy in the beloved. So how much does God love this bride? Here's a short list:

- God starts with the gift of a universe as a stunning witness to who God actually is: Two trillion galaxies, with a few praying mantises thrown in for good measure. As the Hebrew poets say: "The heavens declare the glory of God" (Psalm 19:1).

- When things go wrong with the first family and their offspring, God seeks out a family and raises up a whole nation to be God's bride, to point everyone to the way back to God.

- When this nation does not live up to its calling, God joyfully gives his own son and shows up on planet earth in human skin to make the way back to God. God with us, sure enough—Jesus the Christ, Immanuel.

- When people kill God's own son, God raises him back to life. Having returned to the Father, the Son pours out the gift of God's Holy Spirit on the earth to launch a new age in which everyone following Jesus has God's Spirit filling them with God's life and empowering them as a special gift of God to the world.

- Jesus gathers these people into vibrant, joy-fueled families that together are uniquely gifted to display the life of God in the place they are as a whole ecosystem of God's gifts. As one early Christian writer put it to one such family, "In Christ the fullness of God is presently living in *bodily* form, and that's you all together" (ref. Colossians 2:9).

The trend here is clear. For the bride, God is prepared to give the most precious of all possible gifts—God's own self, over and over again. The greatest gift of God is God.

If a measure of love is the value of the gift, we have every reason to believe we are loved beyond measure. If joy wells up in response to a gift—and the gift we've received is God's own life, then we have access to joy-fuel without end.

Answering the invitation to come and share in the joy of God, this interdependent, interactive family that existed before we did, is the single way that transformation can become sustainable, the one way that we can go the distance in this world and beyond with delight.

You might be thinking at this point, "Awesome thoughts, but it doesn't sound much like what I have experienced so far...why is that?" Great question. So glad you asked!

The gift of God's joy is not forced upon us. It never has been. To that important story, we turn next.

9

Persistent Joy

The Falling Apart of All Things

HUMANKIND IS SMACK DAB IN THE HEART of the great story of history—the invitation to "come and share in our joy." How deeply we embrace this invitation to receive God's delight and to return God's delight, shapes how we see, live and understand the reality around us.

For many of us, parts of our heart cannot even fathom a joy-filled family inviting us to come and share in its delight. Parts of us are stuck in our growing up years experiencing how our parents or caregivers treated us. When we misbehaved, they might have been angry with us and we felt they didn't want to be with us. "Go to your room until you have finished crying!" or "Stop crying or I'll give you something to cry about" might have been your norm. Or perhaps, your caregivers were very difficult to please or even hard to find. Maybe they just weren't there. You did everything right, won so many awards, graduated top of your class, and yet they were still not pleased with you.

This behavior could not be further from God's heart toward us. Yet because of our past history, it will take our hearts some time to fully absorb this fact. So, while we know God is not like that, there are tender parts of our being that only know what we experienced, and unfortunately, that experience or visceral knowing dominates our brain and inevitably our behavior as well.

49

Interestingly, it is not just our broken childhood that may hinder us from understanding and receiving God's love for us, but also how we as Christians use that lens to understand the story told in scripture of when all things fell apart. In particular, our own experience may limit our ability to understand the foundational story that explains why we live in a world with so much pain and so little joy.

Believe it or not, God's delight within himself overflows into a deep delight in us, no matter what. No matter what we are feeling. No matter what we have done. No matter what we *think* we have done.

No. Matter. What.

While we were still sinners, Christ died for us.

Romans 5:8 NIV

This means that even when we were broken and enemies of God, he still saw his image in us. He found so much delight in us and saw so much value in us that He sent His Son to die for us so that we could come home and share in his delight once more.

It is easy to understand joy when all is well and we are getting along. However, to fully grasp this value of being joy-fueled, it is necessary to return to the place where we arrived, smack dab in the middle of the invitation—the falling apart of all things.

The biblical story of the fall is crucial in how we make sense of our world, ourselves and the God who loves us. It will inevitably affect whether or not we can sense the invitation to "come and share" in God's delight when we are at our worst. What does joy look like when we are hurt, angry, wronging someone or being wronged? What exactly happened emotionally and spiritually

50

within the first human family of man and woman? What did they fall from? What happened between them? How did God respond?

So much of the story is not said in the Bible, so we often fill in the gaps with our own understanding of the world. Sometimes we don't even realize we have done this. For example, it may seem like God is angry with Adam and Eve after they eat the fruit, and therefore, he kicks them out of the garden in his rage. Ironically, however, the Bible never says God was angry with them.

Even if God was angry with them, joy is the ability to be glad to be together *even* when you are angry with one another. What would that look like? In reality, we have every reason to believe that even if God was angry, he was still compassionate, grace-filled and forgiving even as he explained the consequences of their actions to Adam and Eve. His character stays the same, even when he is wronged.

The following telling of the fall of man may seem quite different from how Genesis 3 reads. We invite you to play a little with your imagination as we offer a theological-neural approach to what happened in the garden. This is an approach that takes into consideration how our brains were designed to function— with joy being the pervasive emotion. (Refer to the footnotes for the biblical underpinnings for our understanding of this passage's true meaning.)

What Happened at the Fall?

When God created everything, he said, "It is very good." And God placed his image in the man and woman who walked the earth (ref. Genesis 1:26-28; 31).

In the midst of the creation, there was a wonderful garden. It was God's garden of delight and joy, or in their language: *Eden*.

Everything was there, every need met, and it all worked together in peace and harmony. God was with nature, animals and humanity. And all was with God and each other. There was *shalom*—everything in the right place, at the right time, in the right amount, in the right way.

God saw all he had made, and it was very good.

Genesis 1:31 NIV

All the people were also together in one entity called *humanity* or *ha'adam*. They were made in God's image—male and female. They were somehow together in one flesh, naked and unashamed (ref. Genesis 2:24-25).

In the middle of the garden grew two special trees. One tree was about judging right from wrong, good from bad. The other tree was about living forever (ref. Genesis 2:9; 3:22).

God told man and woman they could not eat of the fruit from the tree of judging. If one ate the fruit of the tree of judging good and bad, they would think they could decide for themselves what was right and wrong, and in the end, they would die. However, if they ate from the tree of life, they would live forever.

Now, the serpent was cleverer than any other creature that the Lord God had made. And he suggested to the man and woman that they taste the fruit from the tree of judging.

So they did.

Instead of asking God what he thought about the serpent's suggestion, they decided for themselves. And their relationship with themselves, each other, creation and God fell apart.

Relationship with Themselves Fell Apart.

Their eyes were opened and they experienced reality differently. No longer unashamed, they realized they were naked, and they were struck with fear for the first time in their lives. There was no longer peace or joy within them or between them.

Their Relationship with Each Other Fell Apart.

With sin now distorting their love, God explained that the woman will now experience a new vulnerability and dependence on the man. We see this when Adam, who has been exercising his authority over the animals by naming them, now names the woman *Eve.* And by the next generation, the first murder occurs.

Their Relationship with The Good Creation Fell Apart.

Severed from caretaking the beautiful garden of joy, their existence in creation would now be marked by pain and the sweat of toil.

Their Relationship with God Fell Apart.

Realizing they had decided badly between good and bad, they hid. They were afraid and thought God would be mad at them and reject them. After all, he did say that death would come if they ate of that tree. They did not know how to be with God anymore because they felt afraid and ashamed for breaking their world by not asking for God's perspective and trusting his word.

Before the falling apart, they lived in *Eden*—the joy and delight of God. They never experienced an emotion without God being glad to be with them. Would God still be glad to be with them now? They did not know. They were caught in a complex web of shame, fear and anger.

In God's mercy, however, he called for the man and woman. They hid, but he sought them out. He was still glad to be with them even though there were grave consequences to be faced. He searched for them and found them.

God did not reject Adam and Eve. Even in their shame, fear and anger, his perspective was vastly different than their fallen view of themselves. He still wanted to be with them. He still saw his image in them. They were still priceless to him even though they were broken.

Yes, he showed them the consequences of their decisions. However, like a good father, He was forgiving[1] and

---

[1] We realize this could be a totally different way of seeing this story. You may even say, "Where does the Bible say God forgave them?" While there is no direct statement about God's forgiveness in Genesis, we believe that we can infer His forgiveness based on these facts.

(1) God was gracious to warn Adam about sin and its consequences. God told Adam not to eat of the fruit of the forbidden tree. He told him that if he did, he would die (Genesis 2:15-17).

(2) When Adam sinned, God did not immediately put Adam to death, as his sin deserved. Instead, God sought Adam out, and exposed his sin, which is an act of grace in and of itself (Genesis 3:8-13). God also indicated the consequences Adam and his wife would experience because of their sin, which is excellent parenting (Genesis 3:8-19). God promised to provide a cure for sin and death (Genesis 3:15). He also provided Adam and Eve with coverings, a symbol of love and care, not rejecting or anger (3:21).

(3) God graciously removed Adam and Eve from the garden and prevented them from returning to it. He kept them from eating of the tree of life, lest they live forever in their sin (3:22-24).

compassionate, covering their shame and even making the curse the cure that would crush the serpent and bring humanity back to their father. It is just like God to get so angry that he decides to heal. (Jesus did the same in Mark 3:1-5.) Somehow God stayed relational with Adam and Eve, even in his anger, and he put into motion the plan that would save not just them but all of humanity!

He was glad to be with them no matter what they had done. He was not happy that they chose poorly, but he remained himself in his disappointment. He remained Lover, Creator,

---

(4) God was gracious to turn the curse into the cure. Death kept Adam and Eve from living forever as condemned sinners. It was death (the death of Jesus Christ on the cross of Calvary) that ultimately and permanently defeated Satan, sin, and death because our Lord died in the sinner's place and then rose from the dead. Even the woman's pain in childbearing was gracious, because it was through this painful process that the Messiah would someday come into the world to save sinners.

(5) God graciously gave Adam and Eve another son, Seth, after Cain killed Abel (4:25-26). It was after the birth of Seth that people began to worship the Lord (4:26). Did this include Adam? We are inclined to think so.

All of this suggests that Adam and Eve did seek God's forgiveness, and receive it. The Bible places the emphasis on Adam's sin (and not on his repentance and forgiveness) because it was through Adam's sin that all mankind was corrupted and brought under the same sentence of death (Romans 5:12-21). Adam turns our attention toward the sin of the human race, and God's amazing plan to rescue us.

Father and Savior to them as he drew them out, confronted their sin, met their needs and even provided for their salvation.

This is true joy—to be glad to be with another no matter what they've done, no matter how you feel. Regardless of your feelings, you're glad to be with them because you love each other! This is the powerful joy that made a way for Adam and Eve to forgive themselves, to forgive each other, and to come together again in *shalom*.

They could not go back to when everything was in harmony in the garden. But they could go forward together in a new way, accepting God's invitation to deep joy and relationship with him.

So they did.

In this context, we can more fully appreciate that "while we were still sinners, Christ died for us" (Romans 5:8 NIV). This means that even when we were broken and enemies of God, he still stayed relational with us, still saw his image in us, still found enough delight in us and enough value that he sent his son to die for us so that we could come home and share in his delight once more.

Understanding this depth of joy is a lifetime journey. It is no mere emotion that makes our toes wiggle when someone smiles at us, but a revolutionary act of rebellion against shame and fear that presses into the darkness of our sinful existence to say, "No. Matter. What. I am still glad to be with you. My heart might be breaking over what you have done and are experiencing. I may even be enraged about it. But I am still here, still seeking you out... and I am so angry about what sin is doing to you, to us, to your community and the world around you... so angry, I might just reach out and heal someone or save humanity because that is what I do, even when I am angry."

Why else would Paul pray that "the eyes of your heart may be enlightened in order that you may know the hope to which he has called you" (Ephesians 1:18 NIV). And again in Ephesians, that you "may have power, together with all the Lord's holy people, to grasp how wide and long and high and deep is the love of Christ, and to know this love that surpasses knowledge—that you may be filled to the measure of all the fullness of God" (Ephesians 3:19-20 NIV).

It is this kind of joy that motivated Jesus. In fact, it even gave him the strength he needed to "endure the cross" (Hebrews 12:2 NIV). In our experience, so few of us have actually tapped into this type of joy. However, we are convinced that this is the only fuel that God had in mind to fulfill his redemption of the world.

The lyrics of an old hymn say it this way:

> *Joy in the face of sorrow*
> *Peace in the midst of pain,*
> *Jesus will give, Jesus will give,*
> *He will uphold and sustain!*

Deeper and Deeper
Oswald J. Smith, 1914

Here is the secret to a life of joy in a fallen, broken world. It is participation in the Life of God. It is giving and receiving from a God who loves us no matter what, who is with us no matter what, who is for us even when we are not acting like ourselves, whose image and presence is within us, calling out our worth and value.

Now that we know how important joy is, from before creation all the way to the end of time itself, let's explore more profoundly what we mean by Joy.

10

Joy Defined

Aha! That's It!

John:

I was always confused about joy. It sounded like a wonderful word, but I couldn't figure out exactly what it was. After I became a Christian in high school, I spent a lot of time in the church youth group. The word "joy" would come up in conversation and in Bible study. But, no one seemed to be able to explain what it was or how to get it. In those days, we were taught to be suspicious of emotions. But if it was not an emotion, what was it? I knew it was one of the fruits of the Spirit, but what did that mean?

People could explain what joy wasn't. For instance, they said it wasn't the same as happiness because happiness depends on circumstances. If I got an "A" on a test, I was happy. If I got an "F," I was unhappy. (I knew that feeling well.)

I was relieved when Dr. Wilder, et al. addressed this concern in *Joy Starts Here*. He agrees that "joy cannot be reduced to a feeling that comes and goes." And he goes on to say that "knowing what joy *is not* still leaves people wondering what joy might be" (p. 27).

Some say joy is a choice, yet how can we choose something we do not even understand? In response to this idea, Wilder reviews all of the Christian books that have been written on promoting joy as a choice, and he explains why he disagrees. Joy is relational. It is not something we can just choose; it is something we have to experience within a relationship.

Toni:

Just like John, I was also confused about joy. Even after growing up in an amazing church, graduating with a master's in Christian Leadership Development and serving in ministry for 15 years, joy was still some elusive state that I never knew if I had or not. I knew I was supposed to be joyful as a Christian, but at the same time, like John, I never knew what that was exactly or how to get it. And if I had it, would it take away all of my sadness, anger, fear and shame? Were those negative emotions proof that somehow, I did *not* have joy? Or was it possible to feel those heavy emotions and yet still have joy?

Christian teaching I had heard on joy was actually far from the truth and incredibly harmful. For example, I was taught that joy was an acronym for "Jesus, Others, Yourself." I learned that I was to put myself last in a list of priorities, and that if I did, I would feel joy. I was to attend to Jesus' needs first (as if he needed anything from me!), then other's needs, then my own.

This perspective is so different than thinking that Jesus actually cares about my needs and wants to meet them. Indeed, by ignoring myself, denying my feelings and sacrificially serving others when I was empty, I did not experience joy at all, but burnout and shame for why I wasn't feeling joy!

Joy To The World

Thanks to Dr. Jim Wilder and friends, we finally found a definition of Joy that makes sense:

"Both the Bible and neuroscience understand joy as a relational experience in which someone is glad to be with me" (*Joy Starts Here,* pp. 4-5).

In *Joy Starts Here,* Wilder paints a picture that is extremely helpful. He suggests imagining what a baby does when the mom or dad comes into the room. If there is trust, the baby sees the parent and her face lights up with a big smile. The parent sees the baby's smile and their face lights up too. This goes back and forth between the parent and the child, giving and receiving love. And there we find joy—deep delight! Glad to be with you, not because you did anything, but just because you are. That is Joy!

The greatest gift God can give is God. In the same way, when we bring all of ourselves to others and see them, hear them, understand them and show we are glad to be with them, we bring our best gift. And that gift evokes joy.

At the deepest, most comprehensive level, *joy is our response to a longing fulfilled.*

That bears repeating.

Joy is the response of our whole selves—heart, mind and body—to a longing fulfilled. From the moment we are born, our deepest longing is to be seen, cherished, loved and valued, not for anything we have done but for who we are. The deeper the longing fulfilled, the deeper the joy.

Recall the story of the prayer to see a praying mantis. Little Matty longed to feel special that day, and his delighted squeal on seeing the mantis was the boy's response of joy to that longing fulfilled.

Because we are hard-wired in the image of God, who is love, our deepest longing is for love. Correspondingly, our deepest suffering is the lack or loss of love.

It turns out that this simple description, *joy is our response to a longing fulfilled,* works on so many levels. It is supported biblically and also scientifically by brain science. This fulfilled longing is meant to be the foundation of our relationship with our loved ones and with Jesus as well. It is the source of emotional and spiritual health, and it is the key to creating transformational communities.

Brain science has discovered that the human brain is designed for joy to manage our entire being: mind, will, emotions and body. Joyful interactions with our early caregivers literally shape the structure, chemistry and function of our brain. The foundation of joy that is built in our first year of life has a way of influencing our identity and relationships all the way through adulthood. Without a strong base of joy, many of the God-given capacities we receive at birth will not develop and become strong, except with the intervention of deep healing.

However, as stated earlier, joy is not only felt when people are smiling and approving of us. It goes much deeper. True joy is felt when we have disappointed someone and yet they are still glad to be with us. Or when someone harms us and yet we are still glad to be with them. What would that actually look like and how does joy help us want to be with those who hurt us?

Not many of us have examples of what this looks like, but it is important to hear stories and see examples so that we see different options for how to be with others in a joy-filled way. In Toni's book, *Back to Joy,* there is an entire section of stories where she is struggling with what joy looks like, even when harmed. Here is just one of the stories which gives us a glimpse of how God's delight in us can bring us back to ourselves, even when we are affronted.

Toni:

My parents had just arrived in Uruguay, from the USA. My small children went with me to pick them up from the airport and, as we were returning home, we were affronted by a very rude man. There had been much laughter in our car. Our reunion had sparked story after story of what had happened in our lives in the last six months since we had seen each other. Turning the corner to our street, we saw another car pretty far away driving toward us. Our neighborhood streets only let one car pass at a time, so, as our house was just a few houses up on the left, I thought I could make the turn before the other car got to where we were.

As I approached our house, I noticed that the car in front of us sped up. So I began to slow down to give them the way to pass us. But much to my surprise, the other car had no intention of passing us, and before we could get to my house, the driver intentionally stopped his car directly in front of ours, nose to nose.

We had no idea what was happening. He did not look angry, but also did not make eye contact. In my confusion, I wondered if I had offended this man somehow.

I was not sure what to do. And then, the man turned his car off, leaned over, got his lunch from the passenger's seat, stepped out of the car, closed his door, walked across to the grass, sat down and began eating his sandwich as if nothing happened.

Everyone in my car was dumbfounded. Why would someone treat us this way? I had no idea what was going on in this man's heart, but his actions were extremely confrontational and felt abusive. My dad was in the passenger seat of the car, and I could tell he was fuming.

I quickly prayed, "Jesus help." I took a deep breath, and knowing that my dad did not speak the language and that he would probably let his anger get the best of the situation, I put my hand on his chest and said, "I'll take care of this."

I took my time getting out of the car. I brought to mind beautiful memories of Jesus and me together on a beach. In our quiet times together, I often sensed him there in my imagination. I sensed him dancing with me, holding me. I took a deep breath. His words came to me, "No one can ever take My enjoyment of you away from you." The words and images filled my heart and mind. I let the feeling of his cheek on my cheek calm all my anger. Entering this imaginative memory brought me out of my angry "lizard brain," the part that fights, takes flight or freezes, and into the place where I could remember whose I am, and what it is like my people to do in situations like this. Because I had been practicing staying in appreciation with Jesus, it only took a matter of seconds to connect with him this way, and I could remember that it is like us to bless those who curse us.

I closed my car door calmly, and I walked over to where the man was sitting on the grass. He was definitely shocked that I would approach him with a smile on my face and warmth in my heart, but he just kept eating his sandwich. I could almost feel the pain he was in to act so rudely. I could also feel the deep compassion Jesus had for him.

I sat down beside him, and said in Spanish, "Sir, I'm wondering if I can pray for you today."

"What?" he replied.

I continued in all sincerity, "Yes, I would like to pray for you, because you see, I can only imagine you must be having a difficult day, and I would really like to give to you."

The man didn't know what to say. He looked at me in shock. In Uruguay, aggressive actions are almost always met with anger and confrontation. Here I was a foreigner, and I was not yelling or confronting him, but actually showing him kindness when he knew he deserved anger and hate.

"You can do whatever you want to," he said to me as he shrugged his shoulders apathetically.

I took a deep breath, placed my hand on his back, and asked Jesus to pray through me what this man needed.

Surprisingly, even to myself, words flowed from my mouth in Spanish over this man. I heard myself begging God to bring him and his family to know the deep, abiding love of Jesus. I asked God to bless him with abundant joy and peace.

When I was done, I looked the man in the eyes and he held my glance. I sincerely enjoyed him as a deeply beloved creation of God. Time almost stopped.

Standing to leave, I added, "I hope you have a really good day, sir."

He was stunned into silence.

Upon returning to my car, I could feel the adrenaline getting the best of me. My body was shaking all over. This had been a very painful experience, and while I had stayed relational, and even sensed Jesus with me, my body was carrying the consequences of having been sinned against. Is this what Peter referred to as being a "partner with Christ in His suffering" (1 Peter 4:13, NLT)?

I got back in the car and decided to go around the block to get to my house. By the time I turned the corner to our street, the man's car was gone.

"What did you say to him?" my parents wanted to know. They were angry and shocked. What a welcome this was to Uruguay!

I was still shaking all over and I knew, for my emotional health, that I needed to tell the story. As I recounted what had happened, I sensed God and others validating that what that man did was wrong and hurtful. They all looked at me in the eyes and assured me that I had done nothing wrong. I did not deserve to be treated that way.

I was able to cry and let my emotions come. At the same time, I felt God's pleasure over me for how I had responded to this man.

"You did not forget whose you are!" I sensed Jesus saying. "I want that man to know Me, and today he has experienced My love like never before in his entire life."

Joy Strength

Joy is the only fuel that could motivate someone to "turn the other cheek." No amount of duty or obligation could rewire someone's emotional system in seconds to allow them to sincerely respond by blessing someone who is cursing them. It goes against every natural instinct we have! Connecting to Jesus is our only hope. Sensing him with us, enjoying us no matter what, is the only fuel he meant for us to use when we are challenged to live the life he has called us to live.

When someone is glad to be with us even when we are afraid, the fear is no longer harmful to us. When someone is glad to be with us when we are angry, we calm down and can express it healthily. "Be angry, and do not sin" (Ephesians 4:26 NKJV). When we grieve and yet are accompanied by joy, it actually feels good and honoring to grieve because it lets us feel gratitude for what we have lost. This dichotomy of heavy emotions *and* someone being glad to be with us produces an inexplicable peace. It is a peace that "transcends all understanding" (Philippians 4:7 NIV); a peace we are promised by Jesus himself; a peace that echoes all the way back to the garden of Eden (delight); a peace as *shalom*—

everything in the right place, at the right time, in the right amount, in the right way.

Unfortunately, many of us have rarely, if ever, experienced this type of relationship. Our ability to feel God's joy over us is limited because it lies outside of our physical and emotional experience. We know God loves us, and yet we do not know how to experience that love. So many thoughts swirl in our minds that it's difficult to sense God's thoughts.

Here is where the vital role of quietness comes in to guide us into receiving the peace and joy that is our birthright as Christians. Let's learn more about that elusive yet vital aspect of our relationship with God.

11

Rest and Quiet

How Joy Is Refueled

HAVE YOU EVER TRIED TO SIT IN SILENCE and quiet your thoughts? If you're anything like us, as soon as the external noise stops, the internal chaos rises.

Did I turn off the coffee pot?

That jerk cut me off yesterday!

I can't believe they went behind my back.

Is she gonna leave me?

Should I leave him?

Will I ever find a mate?

Are the kids OK?

Who needs kids anyway?

Did I leave the stove on?

What's for dinner?

Will there be waffles in heaven?

Feelings of inadequacy, fear, anger, worry and culinary angst grip you. With each intrusive thought, your shoulders tense up, your heart rate quickens and your breathing becomes shallower. Thoughts like these rush into the solace and rob your peace.

No wonder we do everything we can to avoid this space. It only reminds us how chaotic and out of control we are. Small wonder that most of us constantly fill the silence with anything and everything from music to food to streaming videos. And with smartphone access just a thumbprint away, we don't *ever* have to be silent. We can even engage with social media or listen to a podcast in the bathroom!

But what if quiet did not have to be chaotic? What if silence became a refuge where we knew how to bring our own internal thoughts, emotions and body sensations into a state of rest? What if quiet could be a mini-vacation where we found deep refreshment whenever we needed it?

> *Surely I have calmed and quieted my soul,*
> *Like a weaned child with his mother;*
> *Like a weaned child is my soul within me.*

Psalm 131:2

Joy and quietness go hand in hand. Joy brings high energy, while internal quiet ushers in a low energy state of rest. When healthy parents enjoy their baby, they also give the baby moments of rest and quiet. Take the game of peek-a-boo for example. This game oscillates between the high joy of saying "peek-a-boo!" and quiet when we cover our eyes and let the baby recover. If we don't let the baby rest, we overstress their central nervous system and cause them discomfort. Believe it or not, even too much joy, when one is not ready for it, can be harmful! The absence of rest, even in the best of times, can be exhausting.

These moments of high joy followed by rest and quiet are essential for trust, growth and healthy development. When joy and quiet are experienced in appropriate amounts, shalom is experienced. Shalom is that powerful rest that comes as we quiet our thoughts, perceive God's presence and know that everything is alright. There is harmony and deep emotional and spiritual safety, even if our physical world is falling apart. Shalom is experienced as the peace "that transcends all understanding" (Philippians 4:7 NIV) that comes to us after sharing our hearts, when we nestle into gratitude and experience God's delight to be with us no matter what we are feeling or what is happening. While it is not the complete journey, learning to quiet ourselves is the first step to enter into that peace. Rhythms of quiet are key to continually refueled lives.

Throughout the Bible, rest and quiet have been linked to the life of God, beginning with God's own rest after creation. Over and over, the people of God are called to God's rest from their own driving agendas. One prophet put it this way:

> *This is what the Sovereign Lord, the Holy One of Israel says: "In turning from your own ways and rest is your salvation, in quietness and trust is your strength."*

> Isaiah 30:15

The same struggle exists today. When it comes to being still, we often don't want to or don't know how to. With all of the external and internal chaos going on, it's hard for us to sense God in quietness. Obviously, we can't control the external noise. However, in learning to quiet our inner worlds, we can learn to sense God's presence and strength in tranquil pools of stillness.

Chris Coursey expounds on this concept in his book, *"Transforming Fellowship: 19 Brain Skills that Build Joyful Community."* He refers to quieting or resting as a skill we develop much like learning a sport or a musical instrument. It is a skill that can be passed on to us by those we spend time with, assuming they have it. However, Coursey reveals that "this skill starts to diminish when families and communities do not allow or have not learned to rest" (p. 59). Without the ability to quietly rest, we overwork, overconsume, overanalyze, burnout, feel depressed and lose the ability to see the internal world of others. Such rest may be one of the most significant skills that we have lost, all but unnoticed, with the demise of the extended family over the past century. So, how do we learn the skill of rest in this frenetic age?

Dr. Allen Schore, a respected researcher in neuropsychology from UCLA, shares that the inability to down-shift into rest and then up-shift into joy lead to the largest risk of developing a mental illness in a lifetime. His extensive study on attachment and emotional regulation points to this powerful synchronized dance between joy and quiet as the source of all resilience and grit (*Attachment, Affect Regulation, and the Developing Right Brain: Linking Developmental Neuroscience to Pediatrics*). Simply put, our ability to quiet our internal world through mental rest is the strongest predictor of life-long mental health.

So, how do we know if we are having problems quieting ourselves? And what can we do to strengthen this skill?

First, as we said, if we do not know how to handle quiet, we avoid silence. This is because, when our outer world is silenced, our inner world becomes louder and demands attention. So, we call a friend, eat chocolate or have a glass of wine. We turn on the radio, the news, a podcast or football game while we cook, drive, work or even use the bathroom. With a backdrop of sound, our minds are occupied enough that we can ignore whatever feelings or thoughts might try to surface.

Now, we are not saying these activities in themselves are harmful. In fact, many of these are joyful activities (especially chocolate). However, if we engage in them in a non-stop fashion, it is a sure sign that we are avoiding quiet.

Why Do We Avoid Quiet?

Again, when the outer world is quieted and our inner world finally gets our attention, we may not like what we hear—thoughts that are often uncomfortable for us, and behind the thoughts, feelings that we deny, hide or numb with substances, people, noise or frenetic activity. These feelings can be hard to articulate but can be sensed behind the thoughts or physical sensations.

Here are some of the thoughts and physical sensations that came this morning in silence:

Fear

How are we going to cover college expenses this semester?

(Tension in the shoulders, shortness of breath.)

Doubt

Are the kids really OK? Have I dropped the ball as a parent?

(Tightness in the chest.)

Insecurity

Did I overstep myself in the meeting last week? Did I hurt anyone? Are they going to reject me? Did I blow it completely?

(An impulse to call a friend to validate me.)

Anxiety

Everything depends on me. What if I fail?

(Heart rate accelerates.)

<u>Shame</u>

Who have I served outside my family lately? I'm useless to society—lazy and selfish. Definitely not "Christian-like" serving the poor. What do I even do that's noteworthy?

(Heaviness throughout body.)

<u>Disconnected</u>

My spouse has been distant all week. I'm lonely and adrift.

(Impulse to plunge into a project and detach.)

These are the thoughts that came in just a few seconds! Who wouldn't want to blast the radio or binge-watch Netflix?

While some emotions surface with words when we quiet the outside noise, others have no thoughts or words behind them. They are primal and can only be detected by paying attention to urges and body sensations.

Maybe you find yourself wanting another coffee. If you can quiet and practice awareness, you can pause to wonder why you want yet another cup. You may sense the words: "Coffee reminds me of my friends. I must be lonely."

Maybe your body feels heavy and tired. Again, pausing to wonder about that, maybe you realize that you are sad about something. Grief robs us of energy and weighs us down.

Grief, loneliness and abandonment are just a few of the emotions that show up in our urges, cravings and body sensations way before we have thoughts or words for them. If we never quiet, we go through life distracting ourselves from these feelings, indulging whatever keeps us from having to pay attention to them. Later we will talk about how to respond to these emotions and thoughts. But for now, we just want to highlight the importance of practicing quiet, rest and silence in the journey towards living joy-fueled.

Learning to Rest

The simplest way to practice rest and quiet is...to rest and be quiet. (Bet you saw that coming.)

Setting your timer to three minutes a day and sitting, being sensitive to what you notice, is the easiest way to practice these skills. The idea is to cease from all work like God did on the seventh day. During this quiet, we pay attention to our bodies, our thoughts and our surroundings. It often feels like a waste of time for those of us who are used to getting our self-worth from producing, achieving and making things happen. Doing nothing, even for a few minutes, goes against everything the Western culture says is important. And yet consistently taking time to sit still is a profound statement that "the world will not fall apart without me," and "I can cease striving and just be."

Some people focus on their breath, some on their bodies and others on something in nature. Whatever you are focusing on, the goal is to be open, meditative, restful and even playful, not solving the world's problems or fixing yourself. You can thank yourself for all of the thoughts, urges and feelings that surface, and then invite them to be still and rest. It takes weeks of practice but eventually the stillness becomes comforting and you can comfortably increase your time.

Other ways to rest alone or in community are working a puzzle together, listening to music, watching clouds, crafting or going for silent walks. Really, anything you might do together, if done in silence, will bring rest as you acquire the skill. These natural breaks affirm that we can just be together without having to work, solve problems or even listen to each other. We can just be.

The Benefits of Quiet

Quiet is the only path to becoming joy-fueled. It is also the most important indicator of mental health. The writer of Hebrews said it best:

> *There remains then, a Sabbath rest for the people of God; for anyone who enters God's rest also rests from his own work, just as God did from his. Let us, therefore make every effort to enter that rest.*

Hebrews 4:9-11 (NIV)

When we grow our ability to rest, we feel satisfied and refreshed. Short moments of quiet provide the resilience and strength for even more joy, which can contain heavier emotions such as grief, shame, anger, despair and disgust. We no longer have to take a defensive posture toward life where we avoid pain and seek pleasure. We use quiet spaces to connect with ourselves and God and can engage with the grief that life brings, matching it with a deep joy—a shalom that "passes all understanding." We become the people God meant for us to be in this world, offering what so many lack—hope. When we develop the skill of quickly quieting ourselves, we grow our ability to stay present with all of our emotions regardless of what is around us. We can sense God's perspective and presence, entering into joy even in the midst of attack.

Consider Stephen's response to a horrific death. Just seconds before, he saw "heaven open up and the Son of Man standing at the right hand of God." Then, instead of crying out in pain and hopeless despair as his persecutors stoned him, he prayed, "Lord

Jesus, receive my spirit... do not hold this sin against them" (Acts 7:54-60 NIV). These were his last words on earth.

If we want to feel loved and love those around us, even those who hurt us, we must train ourselves to do so. This comes from regularly practicing joy *and* quiet through heart-to-heart connection with ourselves, each other and God. It will never come through sheer will or guilting ourselves into it, not through Bible study or studying the martyrs of the faith. That would be like saying we could be pro soccer players because we woke up and chose to play or studied a ton about soccer. Quieting ourselves, returning to joy quickly and sensing God's presence are skills that will only come automatically when we have practiced an ongoing, vibrant connection with Jesus and others, where we can sense him loving us, enjoying us and leading us no matter what.

The invitation to joy is a call to learn the path of rest and quiet. Stillness expands our capacity to receive all that comes our way from God's perspective. It empowers us to respond in God's love and joy. If we want an abundant, joy-fueled life, we must cultivate that space by paying attention to all that goes on within us. This takes practice.

We in LK10 are committed to training people who effectively wield these weapons of joy and quiet, leaders who know how to train others to do so as well.

12

Vibrant Families of Jesus

How Joy Grows

THANKS TO LIFE MODEL WORKS' study and teaching on joy, we now know that this ability to be glad to be with each other no matter what is a skill we can cultivate. It is the result of being in relationship with people who have it. We can practice listening, connecting heart-to-heart, being vulnerable and safe for each other in ways that grow family bonds and nurture a joy-filled life.

Toni:

I began my training with Life Model Works back in 2003. My husband, Matt, and I, were church planters in Uruguay, South America, which at the time had been labeled the "Graveyard for Missionaries" due to the difficult emotional landscape and high levels of depression and suicide. We had sought out Life Model Works' Thrive leadership training in hopes that it would equip us to work in such an emotionally hostile environment. This amazing journey of learning about joy became the framework that brought deep restoration not only among Uruguayans but also in our hearts and the hearts of other missionaries as well.

As we found answers to deal with the emotional difficulties in our family and in the culture, we wondered why these skills were not nurtured in typical church settings. The question burned in us: "If Jesus came to bring joy, and the church is to be his hands and feet to the world, how do we be church to nurture and grow the skills that lead to a life of abundance in Christ?"

For us, there had to be a way of being and doing church that nurtured the relational skills necessary for mental and emotional health.

God heard our hearts' cry, and in 2013 we met John White (of LK10) during a Life Model Works conference call. Ironically, John knew very little about brain science and teachings of Life Model Works and Dr. Wilder. However, it was quickly apparent that the LK10 community was nurturing these skills in the most sacred relationships initiated by God himself: the family.

Church as Family.

John and Kent had discovered a way of being church at a micro-level. They found that listening to God together nurtured the skills necessary to foster joy, quiet, belonging and all of the other relational components of being the people of God that Jesus had in mind when he declared "I will build my church..." (Matthew 16:18 NIV).

Matt and I were amazed and renewed by this. Finally, we could see a way forward to planting a church in Uruguay that would nurture the very skills necessary for emotionally healthy living.

What we learned from John resulted in a change in our paradigm of church. Previously, we believed church was at least 10 adults gathered together to worship, pray and study the Bible. But what if church needed to be even smaller? What if my family of five counted as church? John was relentless in telling us: "Your marriage, followed by your family, is the first and most foundational expression of church. When a couple and their family consistently connect with each other heart-to-heart and connect with God, they become the building blocks of every larger expression of church."

Valuing my husband and family as an expression of church was radically different from what I had known before. It was also simple and transformational. Family and church were not two different things. We didn't have to leave home to "go to church," or sacrifice our family to host a house church. We five people were a valid micro-expression of church. Rather than talking about how to do church in a meeting every week, we began talking about how to be church with each other 24 hours a day.

As we began practicing the unforced rhythms of grace daily (see below), we quickly realized that if we trained people to be a church of two—a micro-expression of church—we would have five micro churches meeting in our home!

At this point, we restructured our ministry to begin training couples to be churches of two. It was not easy at first because we saw how difficult it was for couples to share their hearts with each other. We also discovered that many life-long followers of Christ had no idea how to sense his presence. The gift of focusing on these two skills was life-changing for all. We did not stop with couples but included two friends or a parent and child or siblings. The point was to be a small enough group that heart to heart connection could be practiced as close to daily as possible.

It is a great joy to learn that there is significant historical and biblical support for the idea of church being family. Marvin Wilson, in *Our Father Abraham: Jewish Roots of the Christian*

Faith, reminds us that "Foundational to all theory on the biblical concept of family is the Jewish teaching that the home is more important than the synagogue. In Jewish tradition, the center of religious life has always been the home. The Church has yet to grapple seriously with this crucial concept" (p. 215).

Wilson is convinced that this family dynamic carried forward in the ministry of Jesus and the communities he formed. That thought is echoed by the early church scholar John H. Elliot (*A Home for the Homeless: A Sociological Exegesis of 1 Peter, Its Situation and Strategy*) who points out that "households thus constituted the focus, locus and nucleus of the ministry and mission of the Christian movement." (More on this in our upcoming book about *Ecosystems of Grace*.)

These scholars are not referring to people taking an institutional church culture into a living room. I believe these ancient families were what we call *Vibrant Families of Jesus*— interdependent, intergenerational communities so powerfully sharing physical, emotional and spiritual resources among themselves and the living God that they catalyzed a revolution of joy and peace wherever they went.

Rhythms of Attention.

What made Matt and Toni a vibrant family of Jesus were two simple rhythms of attention. (These are spiritual practices or disciplines.) LK10 refers to these two disciplines as *Checking-in* and *Listening*. These rhythms, practiced daily, turned out to be the key to first nurturing joy and quiet in their own home and then in their extended community.

Both rhythms of attention focus on the heart—the center of our desire and attention. It is when we give attention to heart-level connections and are glad to be with each other that joy grows. While head-level connections (Bible studies, teaching, sermons, etc.) are still important, it is heart-level connections where delight in one another is communicated and character is developed. Our intellectual learning must take place in such holistic environments if we want to fully integrate the learning into our character and see true transformation.

Connecting with Each Other At Heart Level

The first rhythm, *Checking-in*, values connecting with one another on a heart level. This repeated practice is lived out when at least two people take turns sharing with each other how they are feeling and why. Being glad to be with each other no matter what means we resist correcting the other or telling them how they should feel. It means not trying to fix them.

John Eldredge wrote that our "emotions are the voice of the heart" (*Waking the Dead*, p. 42). Sharing our feelings allows us to do what Scripture commands in Romans 12:15: "Rejoice with those who rejoice. Weep with those who weep."

Joy grows as we listen without trying to fix the person or change their feelings or give them advice. They experience being seen, heard and understood, knowing we are glad to be with them no matter how they are feeling.

Kent:

Many years ago, I was working with a troubled mission team in Guadalajara, Mexico. We were taking a few minutes of quiet to reflect with the Lord on what could be done to work through the friction and estrangement the team was experiencing.

83

As we were in the silence, this thought came clearly to mind: *Kent, the pathway to intimacy is mutual self-disclosure.* The truth of that statement hit me like a truck. *Of course! This is a principle I can share with the team. This will teach!*

But that was not the end of it. After a few more moments of silence, this thought followed: *So, when are you going to begin sharing more of yourself with me, so that I can share more of myself with you?* (Of course, *me* was the Lord.)

In the gentle light of that truth, I realized that the same problem troubling this team was stunting my own relationship with God. We were hiding. We were not coming out from behind ourselves to be real. And that failure to get real with each other was holding our relationships at a trite, superficial level, one that lacked the markers of deep love and joy. To move deeper would require mutual self-disclosure.

Getting Real

At one level, it seems that this should be the most obvious and simplest thing in the world to do—just get real with each other. However, we assure you, out of hundreds of pastors and missionaries we have trained over many years, only a handful were even able to share their true feelings with their spouses, much less with others or with God.

So, what keeps people from connecting heart-to-heart?

We could identify many obstacles to the kind of self-disclosure invited by the simple practice of checking in with another person. Here are two.

The first problem is that many of us grew up in homes or churches where emotions were ignored or denied. No one modeled for us by sharing honestly what they were feeling. As we discussed earlier, one of the deep scars left on the church by enlightenment, left-brain thinking is its dismissal of everything that does not compute in its narrow view of reality. So, we minimize emotions, or worse, think they are bad. This type of thinking forms people and cultures with little emotional awareness or understanding.

The second problem is that we don't feel safe sharing our feelings. Most of us are used to getting unwanted advice or even being completely invalidated by being told: "Trust Jesus and it will all be fine." These well-intentioned responses are not usually helpful at all, and in fact, communicate a desire to fix or change the person sharing. What if we could listen without needing to fix, change or make the other person feel better? What if we didn't give input unless the other person asked for it?

Toni:

When Matt and I began checking-in, I realized that his emotions often overwhelmed me, and I wanted to fix him and tell him why he should not feel the way he did. On the other hand, Matt learned that when I shared my feelings, he quickly became overwhelmed and began blaming himself for my grief or disappointment or fear, even when it had nothing to do with him. No wonder we were suffering from low joy!

Through daily practice over the last six years, we have grown the capacity to let the other have their own feelings and to not blame them or ourselves for what the other person is feeling. Also, if heavy emotions are shared, we now anticipate how God is going to speak to each of us in the middle of the struggle. And he always does! This joy, this glad to be together no matter what, has brought about a deep safety in our marriage, giving way to further intimacy. Not only are we vibrant, but we are resilient as well, bearing all sorts of hardship and learning to stay emotionally connected in the process.

As we implemented these changes in Uruguay, church was no longer a physical location but an emotional and spiritual space where people felt deeply seen. They wept with those who wept (ref. Romans 12:15), stayed connected with each other and Jesus, even when they were in pain, returned to joy from negative emotions and sensed God's presence with them individually and communally no matter what. They experienced the Lord leading, guiding, loving and convicting. The more we practiced daily with each other, the more we all grew in our ability to be safe for others.

Connecting with Jesus At Heart Level

Of all the places in our lives, church—the called-out community of Jesus—was meant to be the place where we can share the full range of emotions because we have a God who has felt them all and can handle them. This is why, after checking-in, we turn to our second rhythm of attention: *Listening to Jesus.*

The second rhythm, *Listening to Jesus,* values connecting with God together on a heart level. This repeated practice is lived out when at least two people take time together in silence to sense how God feels about them and discover what God wants them to know about any given subject.

Toni:

When Matt and I began checking in, as I mentioned earlier, it was a little overwhelming for each of us. That is why I am so thankful we quickly learned how to connect with Jesus together. After sharing our feelings, we would thank each other and take five minutes of silence, asking God two questions:

How do you feel about being with us?

Is there anything you would like us to know?

Time after time, we would quiet our hearts and sift our minds for any spontaneous sensations, images, feelings or thoughts that emerged. Even if what we sensed was random and seemingly had nothing to do with anything, we would note it and share with the other.

We discovered that God is incredibly playful and loves to speak to us in community. Matt would get an image; I would get a word. We would evaluate afterward to see if it was consistent with Scripture and brought peace to our souls.

Practicing daily, we trained ourselves to listen to Jesus. Then we trained all of those who were part of our faith community to train in 2's and 3's in similar fashion. LK10 calls these training pairs *Churches of Two* or *CO2s*. We also began to call them *Churches of Few* for those who trained in threes, fours, fives, etc. Our larger gatherings became much more celebratory and vibrant as people came ready to share how God spoke to them during the week, how he challenged them, gave them hope in the face of death or comfort when confronted with abuse or attack. The "teaching time" came from everyone as they shared stories of how they had felt, how they sensed God being with them, and how that changed their feelings and mindset. These families were becoming the very hands and feet of Jesus. At one point, we realized that Matt and I were no longer the leaders. We were all being led by Jesus himself.

Come Together

Being church together in all of its forms should be characterized by connecting individually and communally with God's heart. He loves to be with us, speak to us, comfort us, guide us, correct us, coach us, inspire us, equip us, lead us….

Well, you get the picture.

Most Christians say that they believe in this. However, in our years of training in these rhythms, we have found that most people cannot effectively sense God's presence with them. Some have had moments of clarity when they felt God communing with them or guiding them in important decisions. They remember being "called" into missions or the pastorate or a particular occupation, but these moments were special, once-in-a-lifetime encounters. The idea of sensing God daily, loving them, hearing their emotions and comforting is completely foreign. Many are even too scared to try to commune with God because deep down inside there are fears of being rejected—the same fears that Adam and Eve experienced after they disobeyed in the garden. Even though they know intellectually that they are loved, they cannot feel this love, and so they fear God's anger and rejection, or sometimes worse, God's silence.

On the other side of the spectrum are Christians who only feel God's presence when they have worked themselves up through hours of singing worship music or hearing prophetic words from someone who they believe can hear from God.

While worship and prophecy are beautiful practices within the people of God, the sad reality is that most people have never been taught how to quiet themselves and listen with their hearts to what God is saying to them. Jesus often speaks in a "still small voice" within our hearts as in the story of Elijah (ref. 1 Kings 19:11-13). Here is where that resting, quieting skill enters again, and practice is key. So, we practice listening to Jesus as close to daily as possible, and we practice with at least one other person.

A Word of Caution

Dr. Wilder has personally cautioned LK10 to pay attention to the reality that, at times, many of us wear a "false self" that can hinder authentic joyful community from forming. Our false self is the part of us that we present to others that we think will gain acceptance while simultaneously hiding other facets of ourselves that might be rejected. It is the only side of us we want others to see, the one that has possibly gained us our success in life. It can even be our pain and the way we cope with our pain, especially if fitting in means using substances like drugs or alcohol.

When people's false selves are glad to be together, it is considered pseudo-community (or fake community), and can easily be mistaken for true joy-filled bonds. According to Dr. M. Scott Peck, author of *A Different Drum*, the essential dynamic of pseudo-community is conflict avoidance. Members are extremely pleasant with one another and avoid all disagreements. People, wanting to be loved, withhold some of the truth about themselves and their feelings to avoid conflict. Individual differences are minimized, unacknowledged or ignored. The group may appear to be functioning smoothly, but individuality, intimacy and honesty are discouraged. Generalizations and platitudes are characteristic of this stage.

Interestingly, pseudo-community is actually the first stage of any community. However, if true joyful relationships are to develop, the masks have to come off, disagreement has to happen and the group must move through chaos and disorientation to true community.

In our experience, regularly connecting heart-to-heart with at least one other person, and also listening to Jesus together (through silence, nature, the Bible, etc.), are two practices that invite us out of pseudo-community, plunge us into disorientation and finally bring us to true joy.

LK10, for example, began primarily as a house church network that found itself attracting many who were reactionary against institutional church. They had seen the harm and the ensuing mass exodus, and so were moved to action. Years into training, however, more and more conventional pastors have come to us for training. As we listened to their hearts regarding their congregations, we realized that some of us had attitudes similar to reactive teenagers who bond over hurt, anger and fear. For some, our identity was based on being different than the predominant group in power (the institution). God wanted to heal our church-related pain and help us bond around a joyful identity instead of a painful reactive identity. Today, we love all expressions of church in existence and seek to serve all who call on the name of Jesus, whether they are institutional, organic, a group of a thousand or merely two.

True community is not about agreeing with each other on every issue or railing against those in power. Dr. Wilder reminds us that our true identities are only as strong as how we do at loving our enemies. LK10's daily practices of listening to Jesus together and being vulnerably honest with each other allow us to receive the differences among us, accept God's correctives and let Jesus heal us individually and together.

Can you imagine a whole community of groups of twos and threes gathered who are skilled at sharing their emotions and listening to Jesus together? It is a force to behold, an incredibly powerful and emotionally mature setting, much like 1 Corinthians 14:26 (MSG):

> *When you gather for worship, each one of you be prepared with something that will be useful for all: Sing a hymn, teach a lesson, tell a story, lead a prayer, provide an insight.*

Yet there is also quiet and joy together so no one becomes overwhelmed.

LK10 offers a chance for those who are training with us to experience this at our annual Leader Team Conference. Bringing all of our *churches of two* together to practice being church in this way in a larger setting gives everyone the vision of what we are working for locally. It is truly a taste of heaven on earth and among the most mature expressions of the Body of Christ we, the authors, have ever engaged in. Check out our website (www.LK10.com) for more information about our training resources.

Listening and Prophesy

Sensing God's presence and direction is a skill that is developed by quieting and sifting our imaginations for spontaneous Sensations, Images, Feelings or Thoughts. Hence the term SIFTing. (Thanks to Dr. Dan Siegel for the acronym.)

Of course, there must be balance. Because sensations, images, feelings and thoughts are highly subjective, we are careful in how we speak about what we hear, always weighing it with scripture and in community. That is an important reason we listen in twos or threes. We always cringe when we hear someone declares, "God told me..." or some other equivalent of "Thus saith the Lord!" It seems that this introductory phrase too often is meant to impose authority on the hearers: "What I'm about to say comes directly from God and you had better not question it! I am speaking authoritatively."

In the LK10 Community, we counsel people not to use that kind of language. Instead, we share cautiously so that people will feel free to weigh what is said. "This is what I sense the Lord *might* be saying. Test it and see what you think" (ref. 1 Corinthians 14:29). Even the Apostle Paul's words were tested by the Berean believers, as noted in Acts 17:11.

We also listen in twos and threes because we all perceive God differently. God loves to give one person a word, another an image, another a physical sensation, etc. Altogether, we have the message, yet separately it may seem like nonsense. As we listen together, we see that we really are sensing something from God and not just something insignificant. While we can sense God on our own, by listening and sharing with others, we learn to better distinguish what truly is the voice of God.

These two rhythms of checking-in and listening, practiced as close to daily as possible with at least one other person, connect our hearts together in a beautiful three-way bond with the God of the universe. This experience continually affirms that "I am glad to be with you no matter what." It allows Jesus to lead us as his people. What flows is a revolution of joy and a life of spontaneous mission.

Before we move on to how this revolution spreads, we want to address what happens when people get blocked in their ability to connect with each other and with God. Could there be a microsystem functioning even smaller than a church of two or three? Let's find out.

13

Joy Internal

Cherish Thyself

GETTING REAL, ESPECIALLY WITH OURSELVES, CAN BE TOUGH. Often, how we relate to ourselves actually hinders us from entering into the joy and rest Jesus offers. If we are not glad to be who we are, then it is almost impossible to feel that someone else is glad to be with us.

Toni:

I remember one of the first times I sensed Jesus' presence. As I was meditating on Psalms 45-47, I saw Jesus (in my imagination) standing before me full of honor, beauty, compassion, delight, empathy and fierce devotion. Overwhelmed with awe, I kneeled at his feet. I was so glad to be with him that I was content to stay bowed with my head to the ground and my hands around his ankles. I did not need to see his face.

Jesus, however, did something puzzling. He reached down and tried to gently lift my chin to look me in the eyes. I resisted; I felt too humble. "I can't look at you, Lord! I am not worthy."

Jesus lovingly confronted me. "I have made you worthy, my child. Do you not trust my work?"

I continued to justify my hesitancy. "But I am satisfied with just your feet. I don't need to see you face to face."

Again, Jesus' gentle rebuke came: "That is the problem, my love. You are far too easily satisfied. I have promised you powerful joy and rest... and yet you settle for groveling at my feet. What are you afraid of?"

That's when it hit me. I was ashamed of myself. There were parts of myself that I still hated, parts of me I was embarrassed to let him see. I was so good at looking spiritual and humble, but he could see right through me. He knew that I did not cherish myself. I was still afraid that he would not love the unlovable parts of me that I could not yet find joy in.

"Will you take the risk and let me see you?" He asked softly, as he gently lifted my face upward. As my eyes met his, I let him see me deep within.

Could he really accept all of me? I thought as I studied his face.

Incredibly, I knew he was not ashamed of what he saw in me. On the contrary, his eyes said I was beautiful and worth his love. This was the beginning of me learning to cherish myself.

Worth More

C. S. Lewis saw this same tendency of being too easily satisfied with only a fraction of what God promises:

Indeed, if we consider the unblushing promises of reward and the staggering nature of the rewards promised in the Gospels, it would seem that Our Lord finds our desires not too strong, but too weak. We are half-hearted creatures, fooling around with drink and sex and ambition when infinite joy is offered us, like an ignorant child who wants to go on making mud pies in a slum because he cannot imagine what is meant by the offer of a holiday at the sea. We are far too easily pleased. (*The Weight of Glory and Other Addresses*, pp. 1-2.)

We are far too easily pleased because deep down inside, we do not believe we are worth more. One of the starting places for nurturing a joy-fueled life is learning to cherish ourselves. In other words, learning to be glad to be with ourselves no matter what. We can think of this as internal joy. Because this may be unfamiliar to you, we want to unpack this from a biblical perspective. It may seem strange to talk about being glad to be with ourselves, but this idea of internal joy is hugely important and thoroughly biblical.

Who Are You?

The Bible illustrates the idea that we are made up of several parts. In this way, we are a bit like the Trinity. One person with several parts, multiplicity and unity.

For instance, in Ps. 103:1-2, David writes, "Praise the Lord, O my soul; all my inmost being, praise his holy name. Praise the Lord, O my soul, and forget not all his benefits."

If we ask, "Who is talking here?" the answer is "David."

If we ask, "Who is David talking to?" the answer is "Another part of David that he calls his 'soul'."

The Psalm ends with this same exhortation (v. 22) "Praise the Lord, O my soul." Again, David is speaking to himself.

In Psalm 42:11, we see David having another conversation with his soul. "Why, my soul, are you downcast? Why so disturbed within me? Put your hope in God, for I will yet praise him, my Savior and my God."

In these passages, we see David literally discipling himself. He is paying attention to the condition of his soul and gently asking questions. He is encouraging his soul to remember all that God has done in the past and exhorting his soul to worship God. These Psalms give the impression that David had a regular, ongoing, conversational relationship with his soul.

In Romans 7:21-23, we see Paul's deep frustration with some of his internal parts. *The Message* says it this way...

> *It happens so regularly that it's predictable. The moment I decide to do good, sin is there to trip me up. I truly delight in God's commands, but it's pretty obvious that not all of me joins in that delight. Parts of me covertly rebel, and just when I least expect it, they take charge.*

In 1 Timothy 4:7-8, more of Paul's understanding about internal parts comes to light in his exhortation to Timothy.

> *Train yourself to be godly. For physical training is of some value, but godliness has value for all things, holding promise for both the present life and the life to come.*

For our purposes, the key word in this passage is *yourself.* This is a reflexive pronoun. That means that the subject and the object are the same. If we asked Paul who was doing the training, his answer would be: "I am." If we asked him who was being trained, his answer would be the same: "I am." Paul is exhorting Timothy to train Timothy.

Nurture

Having established the fact that the Bible illustrates repeatedly the idea of having a relationship with our internal parts, we can now look specifically at what that relationship looks like when it is healthy and joy-filled.

In Ephesians 5:28-29 (ESV), Paul describes two key ways a healthy person loves themselves—nourishing and cherishing themselves. He says it this way:

> In this same way (i.e. as Christ loved the church), husbands should love their wives as their own bodies.[2] He who loves his wife loves himself.[3] After all, no one ever hated[4] his own flesh (or himself),

---

[2] **"Bodies."** Note that Paul uses the idea of husbands loving their own bodies and loving themselves as different ways to say the same thing. In other words, husbands loving themselves is not limited to just loving their physical bodies.

[3] **"Himself."** Paul is seeking to help husbands understand how to love their wives. "A husband is to love his wife as he loves himself." The word "himself" is another reflexive pronoun. The one doing the loving of both the wife and the husband himself is the husband. This is, of course, simply a restatement of the second commandment. "Love your neighbor **as yourself**" (Mark 12:31).

[4] **"No one hated themselves."** The word for "hate" in Greek is *mistheo*. It means a negative emotional response towards a person or a thing. In this case, a negative emotional response toward themselves. (Another reflexive pronoun!) The hated thing is decisively rejected; it is detested, the individual

but he nourishes it and cherishes it, just as Christ does the church.

What does Paul mean by "nourishes and cherishes"?

Let's consider *nourishes*.

The Greek word *ektrepho* means "to nourish, nurture, bring to maturity, train, educate."

The remarkable thing is that Paul uses exactly the same word a few verses later in Ephesians 6:4. There it is translated "bring them up." Clearly, in Paul's mind, there is a close connection between how we are nurtured and raised by our parents and how we nurture and raise ourselves.

Fathers, do not exasperate your children; instead, bring them up [ektrepho] in the training and instruction of the Lord.

Ephesians 6:4 NIV (emphasis added).

What we can say is that we learn how to nurture and nourish ourselves based on how our parents did that for us. Some were better than others at this important task. However, we know that there are no perfect parents, so all of us have some deficiencies in our experience of being well nurtured.

---

wants no contact or relationship with it. Of course, we know that it is not literally true that no one hates their own bodies or themselves. Perhaps, to some extent, most of us have negative emotions about some part of ourselves. In extreme cases, people engage in self-harming activities and even commit suicide. In lesser situations, there may be something about our bodies or personalities that we don't like. So, what Paul means is that no one who is emotionally healthy hates themselves.

What this means is that there will be aspects of ourselves that were not well-parented as we were growing up. Those parts of our being may hold immature beliefs about who we are, who God is, and what the world is like.

John:

Many men are taught as boys, either by word or example, to ignore or minimize emotions. This was true for me. As a young adult, I lived life in a very left-brain, task-oriented fashion. I often couldn't even tell you what I was feeling, and I was uncomfortable with people who talked about their emotions. Little by little, however, and with the help of others and myself, that part of me has grown up so that I have a healthier, more mature relationship with my own emotions and the emotions of others. One tool that has helped immensely is LK10's first rhythm of attention—checking in. I now check in on a daily basis with myself, with God and with others.

Cherish

This brings us to the second key word in Paul's statement, *cherish*.

The root meaning of the Greek word *thalpo* is "to warm or to heat." The word is used figuratively "to cherish with tender love, to value highly."

The aspect of physical warmth for this word is conveyed in a somewhat awkward (to us) passage in the Old Testament (ref. 1 Kings 1:1-4). When King David was old, he could never get warm no matter how many blankets were put on him. So his servants found a young virgin to get in bed with him to keep him warm. The Greek word used to translate the Hebrew word for *warm* is the same as above. (The passage hastens to add that David did not have "intimate relations" with the girl.)

A more relevant passage where this same Greek word is used is 1 Thessalonians 2:6-8 (NASB):

> *Nor did we seek glory from men, either from you or from others, even though as apostles of Christ we might have asserted our authority. But we proved to be gentle among you, as a <u>nursing mother</u> tenderly cares for her own children. Having so fond an affection for you, we were well-pleased to impart to you not only the gospel of God but also our own lives, because you had become very dear to us.*

This picture of a nursing mother cherishing her children (used by Paul, a male!) fits perfectly with what we learned earlier about parents and children. Wilder reflects on this when he says, "This is exactly what a baby received from a loving family, total delight that the baby is very special just the way she or he is. No work by the baby is required for smiles, coos, giggles, feeding and Joy" (*Joy Starts Here*, p. 14).

This is clearly what Paul has in mind as he describes how healthy people relate to themselves. They value themselves highly. They take delight in themselves. They treat themselves tenderly and gently. They are glad to be with themselves. They experience internal joy. This is what we see modeled by David in Psalm 139:14 (MSG).

> *Oh yes, you shaped me first inside, then out;*
> *you formed me in my mother's womb.*
> *I thank you, High God—you're breathtaking!*
> *Body and soul, I am marvelously made!*

I worship in adoration—what a creation!

John:

I realize that cherishing myself is not something that I've done well for much of my life. One of my internal parts is a sort of critic. His role is to point out things that I didn't do well, like an assignment that I didn't complete on time, an unkind word that I spoke to someone. This part of me also reminds me of areas where I've failed as a husband, as a father, as a friend, as a follower of Jesus. My inner critic has been fulfilling his role for a long time and is quite good at what he does.

What I'm learning to do, with Jesus' help, is to appreciate my critic. He actually means well and sometimes provides a necessary perspective on my life. However, he can also create lots of anxiety and discouragement. So, I'm learning to ask him at times to step back and invite other parts to celebrate things they have done well in the course of a day when:

- I did a good job of listening to my wife.
- I encouraged one of my daughters.
- I effectively facilitated a group.
- I connected closely with Jesus.

I relate to my inner critic as I would a child, appreciating what he is trying to do, i.e. making me a better person, while at the same time gently inviting him to see that there might be a better way to motivate me some of the time. When I do this, my critic relaxes and is more willing to let in other perspectives from other parts of me. He is also more able to listen to Jesus.

Reparenting

It would appear that good self-care is ideally learned by receiving it as children and seeing it modeled by those around us. So, how do we learn to nurture and cherish ourselves if our parents were lacking at it? What if we learned instead to shame ourselves, hate ourselves (or parts of ourselves), and think of ourselves as worthless, bothersome and unwanted?

In our experience, learning to care for ourselves and cherish ourselves has come as we have let ourselves be reparented. Yet this begs the question: Who reparents us? Thankfully, there are several key relationships where we have found effective reparenting happening in our own lives:

God as father who cherishes me.

This is the starting place. Like Toni's earlier story, God wants to reparent us and show us how valuable we are to Him.

We see God as a parent in his relationship to his son, Jesus. In Matthew 3:17 (NIV), he says of Jesus, "This is my Son, whom I love: with him I am well pleased." If we apply what we know about good parents, we would conclude that this probably wasn't the only time that the Father communicated to Jesus that he was a source of delight to him. And, since we know from Romans 8:29 that Jesus was the firstborn among many sons/daughters (that's us!), it follows that this Father (like any good father) desires to remind us daily that we are his kids, that he loves us and that he is pleased with us. Of all the fathers in the universe, our Father in heaven is the one that is best at doing what Paul described in

Ephesians 6:4: "Fathers, nurture and nourish your children and help them grow up."

It doesn't take much. We may feel that we must accomplish great things before the Father would be pleased with us. But, in Matthew 25:23, Jesus tells us that the Master affirms the servant who is faithful in only a few things. "Good and faithful servant!" (Luke 19:17 says just "one small thing.") And even more, the master invites the servant to "come and share in your master's joy." All that for being faithful in just a few small things.

Henri Nouwen understood that God is a father who cherishes us. He wrote:

> The real "work" of prayer is to become silent and listen to the voice that says good things about me... Self-rejection is the greatest enemy of the spiritual life because it contradicts the sacred voice that calls us the "Beloved." Being the Beloved expresses the core truth of our existence. (Life of the Beloved: Spiritual Living in a Secular World)

Spiritual mothers and fathers in my life.

These are mentors who feel drawn to intentionally cherish us and meet some unfulfilled parenting needs. God often orchestrates spiritual adoptions in our lives where we find the joy and shalom to heal and grow. Jesus was this kind of spiritual father to the disciples, reparenting them during the three years he lived with them (ref. John 14:9).

Paul and his apostolic team functioned the same way.

We were gentle among you, like a mother caring
for her little children. We loved you so much that
we were delighted to share with you not only the

105

*gospel of God but our lives as well, because you
had become so dear to us.*

1 Thessalonians 2:7-8 NIV

*For you know that we dealt with each of you <u>as a
father</u> deals with his own children, encouraging,
comforting and urging you to live lives worthy of
God, who calls you into his kingdom and glory.*

1 Thessalonians 2:11-12, NIV

In LK10, we feel this concept is so important that we have
made it one of our Five Core Values. (We will develop this in an
upcoming book.) This training of spiritual moms and dads is a vital
aspect of what church looks like when Jesus is the leader.

<u>Brothers and sisters (biological and spiritual)</u>.

Our siblings can cherish us and remind us who we are. These
are not just people we go to church with, but friends who have
our backs no matter what. We have high trust relationships and
access to each other's hearts. They know our true identity and
design and often celebrate us when we live and act from that
place. We often hear people saying things like: "You know, it's just
like you to be generous like that!" They also are there to gently
remind us who we are when we are not living out of our true
hearts. "That's not like you to close yourself off from everyone
else. What's going on?"

<u>Cherishing myself</u>.

Parts of ourselves that are more joyful and mature can
reparent other parts of us that are stuck. We can grow in our
ability to have inner conversations that nurture ourselves and
show us we are glad to be with us, even when we are hurting, sad,

overeating, lazy, overwhelmed, etc. A simple starting place is to ask ourselves questions like:

- What part of me do I need to pay attention to today?
- What did I do well today?
- What is there about myself that I can delight in?

First Thing Every Day

In the 1800s, George Muller was one of the best known and most loved Christian leaders in the world. During his life, he traveled over 250,000 miles and shared principles of faith with more than three million people. Without ever asking for money, by faith, he built orphanages that cared for two thousand homeless children. How did he do it? Here is the secret that he learned early in life.

> "I saw more clearly than ever, that the first great and primary business to which I ought to attend every day was, to have my soul happy in the Lord. The first thing to be concerned about was not, how much I might serve the Lord, how I might glorify the Lord; but how I might get my soul into a happy state, and how my inner man may be nourished... How different when the soul is refreshed and made happy early in the morning, from what it is when, without spiritual preparation, the service, the trials and the temptations of the day come upon one." (*Autobiography of George Mueller* compiled by Bergen, pp. 152-154)

Because we believe that being reparented is key to living in joy-filled relationships with God and others, our training in LK10 focuses on listening deeply to ourselves, each other and Jesus. As a Christian, these are the most important skills to learn.

Everything else stands or falls on this ability to listen (pay attention) to our hearts, God's heart, and the hearts of those we walk with. All of the courses and coaching offered by LK10 seek to remove what hinders us from listening to God and our hearts, strengthen the relational mental skills necessary to listen well, and provide community structures and practices that nurture this listening through continued practice.

As you can see, cherishing ourselves is a crucial aspect of nurturing a joy-fueled life where we can enjoy God and be enjoyed *by* God and others. The same practices of checking in and listening can be used to grow inner joy as we learn to dialogue with ourselves. Connecting heart-to-heart with a few others and God amplifies the joy strength and lets Jesus lead us as his people. As families and small communities grow their capacity to be "glad to be with you no matter what," and let themselves be coached, loved and led by Jesus, what follows is a revolution of joy and a life of spontaneous mission. But how does this revolution spread? If we don't guilt people into sharing their faith, how will the good news spread?

Let's see what mission looks like from a joy-fueled narrative.

14

Spontaneous Joy-Fueled Revolution

Changing the World

THE JOY-FUELED REVOLUTION is self-propagating exactly as Roland Allen described in his book: *The Spontaneous Expansion of the Church.* When people pay attention to their own hearts and the hearts of others and Jesus' heart, joy spreads from one person to the next and from one family to the next like a benevolent virus.

We have hundreds of stories that illustrate the spontaneous nature of this revolution. Here are a few:

- Gloria in Honduras, who has taught 600 teachers how to check in with their families and colleagues.

- A conventional church in Massachusetts that has been transformed in the last year as more than half of the members have learned the rhythms through Church 101.

- Terrance in Colorado, who has finally learned to hear God's voice after believing in him for 40 years!

- Jen in Thailand, who has taught the rhythms to dozens of inmates in the local prison.

- Jim and Cathy in Texas, who have taught their 17 grandkids how to check-in and listen to Jesus.

- The 100 pastors in Uganda, who are now checking in with their wives and listening to Jesus together for the first time.

- Nigel in Ireland, who is seeing his immediate family, nephews and nieces being touched by the Lord through the simple rhythms learned in C101.

- Karolina, a 16-year-old in Russia, who experienced a depth of community that she never knew existed.

- Marty, who found a way to coach, train and care for all of the Central American missionaries under his leadership.

- Colleen, who has taken the rhythms into college ministry where she is seeing heart-to-heart connection happening with college athletes.

This revolution is both qualitative and quantitative. Lives are being transformed as a growing number of people are invested in the community. It is impacting both Christians and not-yet-Christians. The revolution is transcultural, spreading effortlessly to countries all around the world, affecting young and old, men and women.

All of this is taking place apart from the gospel of knowledge and duty. There are no exhortations to get busy fulfilling the Great Commission. There is no central plan or strategy other than teaching people to connect on a heart level with each other and with Jesus.

Back in our early days before LK10, our discipleship program was: "Listen to Jesus, obey and teach others to do the same."

Now in LK10, we say: "Listen to Jesus and receive what he says."

Everything flows from listening—church, family, missions, etc. (Watch for our next book, which is about being Jesus-led.)

To be clear, we are still big fans of obedience to Jesus. The problem with our earlier statement, however, is that it implies that the main outcome of giving the Lord our attention is his next assignment for us. But that expectation is so far short of what Jesus is offering—sharing the attention of our God who is love! Whatever God wants to share with us *is* the agenda, not merely an assignment. We want to receive with open hearts and no preconceived agenda.

The two rhythms of attention—checking in and listening—are simple because, as Neil Cole says, "Only that which is simple can multiply rapidly."

And that is what we are seeing, a sort of viral multiplication. Once a person learns the rhythms, they are equipped to train others. Who wants to do rhythms alone? And, they are not just for adults. Children learn them easily.

This viral multiplication is exactly what happened with the early church. Biblical scholar, Robert Banks suggested that the "early church conquered the Roman Empire one household at a time" (*The Church Comes Home*, Robert and Julia Banks, p. 64).

Roland Allen, reflecting on what he saw in the early church, wrote: "I know not how it may appear to others, but to me this un-exhorted, unorganized, spontaneous expansion has a charm far beyond that of our modern highly-organized missions" (*The Spontaneous Expansion of the Church*, p. 7).

One more thing.

Beyond the two rhythms of attention, there is also something called "the 10:2b Prayer" that Jesus has invited us into. It has been the source of great joy and great fruit. Below, John shares how God coached them in the beginning.

John:

One day, about 20 years ago, I was having breakfast with my friend Kenny Moore. At that time, Kenny worked for a major denomination and had responsibility for church planting in Colorado. Over breakfast, Kenny was bemoaning the fact that the traditional method of planting churches was frustratingly slow, difficult and expensive. Estimates of cost for a traditional church startup varied greatly but it was often in the hundreds of thousands of dollars (https://missionalchallenge.com /how-much-does-it-cost-to-start-a-church/). It was necessary to find a charismatic personality who could attract crowds, find land to build a building or money to rent a facility, figure out parking and permits and advertising and furnishing...on and on.

Kenny and I had heard about church planting movements in other parts of the world where dozens or even hundreds of churches were planted in a short period of time. But how could that happen in the U.S. without having to embrace a highly programmed, gospel of knowledge and duty type model?

At that time, we had discovered the importance of Luke chapter 10 as a description of Jesus' strategy (even though the LK10 Community was several years in the future). Over breakfast, we were pouring over that chapter when my attention was drawn to verse 2. I could see the picture in my mind. There was Jesus standing in front of 84 of his disciples.[5] He was about to send them out by twos to "every town and village where He was going." Their assignment was to find a "house of peace" in each town and to impart the Kingdom in that household. (We think they were planting house churches.)

What got our attention was what Jesus said in verse 2. "The harvest is plentiful but the laborers are few."

What?! Jesus had 42 church-planting teams and his assessment was that they were few? That was astonishing to us. Kenny and I would have been thrilled with 42 church-planting teams in Colorado.

Then in the second half of verse two, Jesus told the 84 how to get more church planters. "Therefore, beseech the Lord of the harvest to send (more) workers to his harvest field."

I looked at Kenny and said, "What if we tried praying this prayer that Jesus instructed here? What if we prayed this prayer together every day for a week (being great men of faith!) for the state of Colorado just to see what would happen? I'll call you or you call me and we'll pray over the phone."

Kenny said that he was up for the experiment.

We got about three days into praying what we began calling "The 10:2b Prayer" and we realized that we had no idea how to pray it. Do we just say, "John and Kenny

---

[5] Verse 1 says "Jesus called 72 others." It's likely that this meant 72 in addition to the original 12.

here; Lord of the harvest, please send more workers"? Is that it? Our confusion prompted another prayer. "Holy Spirit, teach us how to pray this prayer." That second prayer launched us into one of the greatest adventures of our lives.

Kenny and I ended up praying and listening together almost every day for the next seven years. The Holy Spirit taught us many insights through that verse. And the best thing was that we found that the Lord of the harvest actually did answer the prayer that Jesus taught his disciples. Through all kinds of circumstances, people who were already motivated to start a church began to appear. They were already prepared and just needed a little training. The Lord of the harvest had done all the work inspiring, motivating, and calling. Church planting became amazingly simple, easy and joyful. Kenny began to say, "Jesus did the heavy lifting."

When you pray one prayer every day for seven years, it begins to change your mindset. We began to anticipate answers to that prayer. In every situation, we looked to see if there were people who the Lord of the harvest had sent out. They began to appear on a regular basis. We found ourselves in the midst of spontaneous divine appointments over and over again. In addition, we began to see the critical role that praying for harvest workers and listening to God's perspective played in the multiplication of Christ communities.

"The 10:2b Prayer" became such a joyful experience that we included it in Church 101 and began teaching it to others at every opportunity. Praying for God to send laborers, and training those he has prepared, are being

114

practiced by leaders all over the world. As a result, leaders are trusting God to do the heavy lifting. Thousands of churches, a.k.a. vibrant families of Jesus, have sprung up around the globe.

The spontaneous, joy-filled expansion of Christian community is not only possible, it is a reality. People are finding hope and empowerment to join God in revitalizing all expressions of church. Not out of duty or obligation or the will of man, but out of heart-to-heart connections that overflow to those around us. Jesus is inviting all of us to join him in this revolution of joy. What holds you back from Joining him?

15

A Story to Join

Where Do We Go from Here?

IN 2003, CHURCH CONSULTANT REGGIE MCNEAL WROTE:

> A growing number of people are leaving the institutional church for a new reason. They are not leaving because they have lost faith. They are leaving the church to preserve their faith.

> The current church culture in North America is on life support. It is living off the work, money, and energy of previous generations from a previous world order... The imminent demise under discussion is the collapse of the unique culture in North America that has come to be called "church." This church culture has become confused with biblical Christianity, both inside the church and out. (*The Present Future: Six Tough Questions for the Church*, p. 1, 4)

What McNeal predicted in 2003 was increasingly true in 2015 when Packard and Hope reported on their research of the Dones. Today, we see no indication that this trend is changing.

Jim Wilder offers a similar perspective...

> Many Christians and their children have noticed that the things of God do not move them, leave them flat and even lower their joy. For about the last 400 years the church has tried to restore Christian Character through

117

education, right beliefs and right choices... (But) because of the lack of real character change, many simply leave the church. Many who stayed in the church struggle with low joy while others are phony or unpleasant. (*Joy Starts Here*, p. 151)

When people are leaving the conventional church in mass because they are trying to preserve their relationship with God, something is not right.

What are we going to do about this?

The sad reality is that few who leave find a better story to join. They feel isolated and alone. Some may have a house church or live church as family, but most do not belong to anything bigger than themselves.

What if we could be church where:

- heart-to-heart connection and mission are possible?
- character change is both viral and sustainable?
- transparency and authenticity are the norms?
- we belong to a family that has our back no matter what?
- we have the skills to handle maturely whatever disaster comes our way?
- we have the spontaneity to follow wherever the Spirit leads?
- it is both micro and global at the same time?
- we can be diverse in our backgrounds and cultures and yet unified in our values and practices?

This is not just a dream. Being church in this way is LK10's reality.

We are calling for the Bride of Christ to reclaim the story that God is telling, and for her to say "Yes!" to God's invitation.

Come, share in our delight!

God is inviting us into deep delight. He is inviting us to live as vibrant families of Jesus. At its foundation, church is meant to be interdependent communities of practice, powerfully sharing resources (relational, spiritual, and physical) between themselves and the "God who is with us," catalyzing a self-propagating revolution of joy and peace wherever they go.

Don't you want to be a part of that revolution? Jesus is still initiating this radical paradigm shift and inviting us to join him.

We are calling on the Dones to rise up, enter into God's deep delight and be open and willing to reconceive and recreate church instead of abandoning it. God is calling you, those who have left, into something much larger than you could imagine.

For those who are still working within more traditional churches, your patience, tenacity and restorative spirit is a deep manifestation of the heart of God. We hope to support you with all the resources you need to stay joy-fueled as you attempt to create a culture change from within. That is no small task, and one that can only be done with a great source of joy at hand.

The invitation stands.

He awaits your response.

Stay tuned...for our next book:

Jesus Led

Because Jesus desires to have an intimate, conversational relationship with his followers (John 10:27), we train ourselves to relentlessly listen to him individually and with others. From our family meals all the way to our board meetings, regarding every single aspect of our lives and work, we ask, "Jesus, what do I/we need to know about this?"

We seek to listen and follow what we learn from him.

Recommended Resources for Further Growth

Training Resources

The LK10 website: www.LK10.com

Nurturing Joy and Other Relational Brain Skills

- *Joyful Journey: Listening To Immanuel,* E. James Wilder, Anna Kang, John Loppnow, Sungshim Loppnow. This is a great starting place. A short practical book on how to connect closely with Jesus and how to nurture joy in your own life and in a group.

- *Transforming Fellowship: 19 Brain Skills That Build Joyful Community,* Chris M. Coursey. The title speaks for itself.

- *The Life Model: Living from the Heart Jesus gave you,* James G. Friesen, *E. James* Wilder, Anne M. Bierling, Rick Koepcke, Maribeth Poole. This is a short introduction to a unifying approach to wholistic Christian living and ministry. Great discipleship tool for starters.

- *Joy Starts Here: the transformation zone.* E. James Wilder, Edward M. Khouri, Chris M. Coursey, Sheila D. Sutton. Feels like it was written by a committee so the structure is a bit confusing but lots of great insights.

- *RARE Leadership: 4 Uncommon Habits for Increasing Trust, Joy and Engagement in the People You Lead,* Marcus Warner and Jim Wilder. Relational brain skills applied to leadership.

- *The Solution Of Choice: Four good ideas that neutralized Western Christianity*, Marcus Warner and Jim Wilder. A small book that explains why only family-like attachment groups produce sustainable transformation.

- *Back To Joy: An Intimate Journey With Jesus Into Emotional Health And Maturity,* Toni M. Daniels. Not another how-to, this book gives you an inside understanding of what it looks like to find your way back to joy.

- *Grow Where You're Planted: Collected Stories on the Hallmarks of Maturing Church,* Edited by Daniel Steigerwald and Kelly Crull. See the chapter titled Cultivating Missional Hearts, for Toni and Matt's full discussion of mission.

Church as Family

- *House Church and Mission: The Importance of Household Structures in Early Christianity*, Roger W. Gehring. A doctoral-level book that demonstrates biblically and historically that "households thus constituted the focus, locus and nucleus of the ministry and mission of the Christian movement." A very important book! But, not easy to read. Before you buy it, email John and ask for his summary of the book. (John.LK10@gmail.com).

- *When the Church Was a Family*, Joseph H. Hellerman. A traditional pastor seeks to implement this idea in his church.

- *Houses That Change The World: The Return Of The House Churches,* Wolfgang Simson. A revolutionary book that got John started on this path in 1999.

- *Stories of God at Home: A Godly Play Approach,* Jerome W. Berryman. Answers the questions, "What do we do with children? And How do we best nurture their spirituality?"

Roland Allen

- *The Compulsion of the Spirit,* A Roland Allen Reader Edited by David Paton and Charles H. Long. A fairly short anthology of Allen's best writing. This is a good place to start.

- *The Spontaneous Expansion of the Church,* Roland Allen. Perhaps Allen's best-known book. Written in 1927, it's not an easy read but is worth the effort. You can find it for free at various places on the web. Here's one: https://www.gospeltruth.net/allen/spon_expanofch.htm

- *Missionary Methods: St. Paul's or Ours?,* Roland Allen. The title gives you a hint as to why it was so controversial to many missional leaders.

Internal Family Systems

These are some resources that have helped us learn how to enjoy ourselves:

- Center for Self Leadership https://www.selfleadership.org/. This is an approach to counseling and personal growth that begins with the idea of multiplicity within each of us. Also called Internal Family Systems Therapy (IFS).

- *You Are The One You've Been Waiting For,* Richard C. Schwartz. Very helpful IFS approach to marriage.

- *Boundaries For Your Soul: How to Turn Your Overwhelming Thoughts and Feelings into Your Greatest Allies*, Allison Cook, PhD and Kimberly Miller, MTh, LMFT. A Christian approach to IFS. Very practical.

Some of John's favorite quotes and things that didn't make the book

- In Chapter Three, we talk a lot about the word "knowledge." Here's a helpful article that gives the perspective of Biblical Hebrew through a word study of the Hebrew word *yada*: https://www.chaimbentorah.com /2016/11/word-study-an-intimate-knowing- %D7%A2%D7%93%D7%99/

- More from Jim Wilder on why biblical knowledge alone doesn't change lives...

The slow-track part of our brains can analyze information about the life of Jesus and be inspired by it, but by itself, the slow track cannot change our identity. Simply knowing the truth about how Jesus modeled godliness does not make us godly. For example, Isaiah knew that God was holy, but it was not until he encountered this transcendent God that his identity changed. Interacting with a holy God made Isaiah aware of his own sinfulness and, interacting with a holy God healed and transformed him. (*RARE Leadership*, p. 54)

More of Roland Allen's perspective on the Great Commission. From *The Ministry of the Spirit*.

Acts does not begin with "The Lord Jesus said, 'Go'"; but with "You shall receive power, and ye shall be witnesses." St. Luke fixes our attention, but not upon an external voice, but upon an internal Spirit. This manner of command is peculiar to the Gospel. Others direct from without, Christ directs within; others order, Christ inspires; others speak external words, Christ gives the Spirit which desires and strives for that which He commands; others administer a dead letter, Christ imparts life... (Luke) speaks not of men who, being what they were, strove to obey the last orders of a beloved Master, but of men who, receiving a Spirit, were driven by that Spirit to act in accordance with the nature of that Spirit (p. 5).

Christ had given them a world-wide commission, embracing all the nations; but intellectually they did not understand what He meant... They did not base their action upon any intellectual interpretation of the nature and work and command of Christ... The apostles acted under the impulse of the Spirit; their action was not controlled by the exigencies of any intellectual theory. This is most manifest in those steps towards the evangelization of the Gentiles upon which St. Luke lays special stress... St. Peter certainly did not think the matter out, decide that the Gentiles were within the terms of Christ's commission, and then, and therefore, proceed to preach to them (pp. 46-47).

More from John Piper in *Future Grace*

It is remarkable how widespread and durable the debtor's ethic is among Christians. Recently I heard a well-known evangelical leader deliver a powerful message about the need for Americans to recover the call of duty and devotion to Christ. He used a compelling illustration about self-sacrifice. But his explanation of the spiritual dynamics of the sacrifice focused entirely on gratitude for what Christ had done.

This way of motivating duty and devotion seems harmless, even noble. Its appeal is strong. It speaks in words that are almost above criticism. For example, it might say, "God has done so much for you; now what will you do for him?" Or: "He gave you his very life; now how much will you give to him?"

This appeal to gratitude as a way of motivating Christians is so common it may come as a shock when I question whether it has much biblical support... this way of thinking seems almost totally lacking in the Bible... This is stunning when you let it sink in. This most common way of talking about motivating Christian obedience is scarcely mentioned in the Bible. This fact comes like a punch in the belly; it takes your breath away. Is this really so? You will need to search for yourself to be completely sure (pp. 32-34).

More from John Piper on being motivated by duty vs. spontaneous affections from *Desiring God*

Worship is a way of gladly reflecting back to God the radiance of his worth. This cannot be done by mere acts of duty. It can be done only when spontaneous affections arise in the heart.

Consider the analogy of a wedding anniversary. Mine is on December 21. Suppose on this day I bring home a dozen long-stemmed red roses for Noel. When she meets me at the door, I hold out the roses, and she says, "O Johnny, they're beautiful, thank you," and gives me a big hug. Then suppose I hold up my hand and say matter-of-factly, "Don't mention it; it's my duty."

What happens? Is not the exercise of duty a noble thing? Do not we honor those we dutifully serve? Not much. Not if there's no heart in it. Dutiful roses are a contradiction in terms. If I am not moved by a spontaneous affection for her as a person, the

128

roses do not honor her. In fact, they belittle her. They are a very thin covering for the fact that she does not have the worth or beauty in my eyes to kindle affection. All I can muster is a calculated expression of marital duty (pp. 72-74).

Great quotes on joy from *Joy Starts Here* by Wilder, Khouri, Coursey, Sutton

Joy is relational. Joy is contagious. Joy is transforming. Joy starts with a smile. Joy helps our brain grow better than any health food. Joy reduces stress. Joy has more social impact than looking sexy. Joy improves our immune system more than exercise. Joy protects marriages. Joy raises brighter, more resilient children. Joy improves resilience after disasters. Joy spreads to transform lives (p. 4).

A quick look at how our brain develops gives us a hint of why God rewards us with joy. The capacities and chemistry that we use as infants become the dominant systems for our brains.

Joy makes us grow strong, loving relationships with other people. We love as a response to joy. Joy stimulates the growth of the identity region of our brains. We grow the strongest and most stable identity from those who show us joy.

Joy is a high-energy state for the brain. The practice of joy builds brain strength and the capacity to engage life with energy, creativity and endurance. In fact, the capacity for the brain to engage every intense or difficult aspect of life develops out of joy. High-joy people are very resilient. High-joy communities are energetic and productive even in hard times. When we are empowered by joy, we are able to suffer, withstand pain and still maintain intact relationships with other people. Without joy, we view problems as "win or lose" situations, and solve problems by choosing the option that causes us the least amount of pain, usually at the expense of others. With joy, we are empowered to find creative, mutually satisfying solutions for problems and love to create simply because we can. Dancing, gardening, feasting, celebrating, playing and other endless good things bubble up from joy (p. 8).

When we are the sparkle in someone's eyes, their face lights up with a smile when they see us. We feel joy. From the moment we are born, joy shapes the chemistry, structure and growth of our brain. Joy lays the foundation for how well we will handle relationships, emotions, pain and pleasure throughout our lifetime. Joy creates an identity that is stable and consistent over time. Joy gives us the freedom to share our hearts with God and others. Expressing our joyful identity creates space for others to belong. Joy gives us freedom to live without masks because, in spite of our weaknesses, we know we are loved. We are not afraid of our vulnerabilities or exposure. Joy gives us the freedom from fear to live from the heart Jesus gave us. We discover increasing delight in becoming the people God knew we could be. (Wilder, *Joy Starts Here*, p. 35)

Joy is relational. It is when two or more people are delighted to be together. Joy grows out of love bonds and tender responses to others. Joy helps people discover who they really are, build strong bonds, develop character, resolve traumas, overcome problems and develop the relational joy skills we call maturity (p. 55).

More from John White:

In Chapter 12, I introduced the *10:2b Prayer* (from Luke 10:2) as a key element in the expansion of the early church. I've gone into much greater detail about this prayer in an article that I call "The Jesus Strategy" (https://lk10.com/the-jesus-strategy/). We have been praying this prayer for almost 20 years and believe it is just as important today as it was when Jesus first introduced it to his disciples.

About the Authors

JOHN C WHITE, host of the podcast, *Stories of the Revolution*, is a spiritual entrepreneur and Co-founder of LK10.

A graduate of Washington and Lee University (BA in Sociology) and Fuller Seminary (MDiv), John served as an ordained Presbyterian pastor (EPC) in three churches over the course of 25 years in Denver, CO. In 1998, the Lord moved him out of conventional church and into the fledgling world of house churches, where he served as a house church coach and as US Coordinator with DAWN Ministries for six years.

As the LK10 Vision Champion, John was the original designer of both the Church 101 Course and Leader 101. Since 2008, those Courses have been responsible for training more than 5000 people in 30 countries in the skills necessary for forming, nurturing, and reproducing vibrant families of Jesus. John can currently be found training, coaching, and facilitating live video calls and connecting with leaders around the world on the latest messaging apps.

John and his wife, Tamela, enjoy their three grandkids, playing tennis, and eating the delicious Albanian food Tamela cooks. While they have lived in Denver, CO for most of their married lives, they recently moved to Naples, FL for the warm weather and to be closer to family. They will however, still be rooting for the Denver Broncos! John can be reached at John.LK10@gmail.com and through his podcast *Stories of the Revolution*.

 TONI M DANIELS is a bilingual leadership coach, ordained minister, pastoral counselor and author of *Back to Joy: An Intimate Journey with Jesus into Emotional Health and Maturity.*

Before settling stateside Toni worked with her husband Matt as a social entrepreneur, church planter, and relational skill coach for 18 years in Uruguay, South America where they co-founded The Geronimo Center for Innovation and Leadership. Toni currently harnesses all of her experience in her role as LK10's Training Champion.

Toni has a BA in Sociology from the University of Memphis, an MA in Leadership Development and Church Planting from Columbia International University, a diploma in Spiritual Direction from La Universidad Catolica, and a total of five years of skills-based relationship enhancement training from the International Trainer's Association, PREP,inc., and ThriveToday.

Toni loves being outdoors and spending time building joy with family and friends, especially her husband, their four children, and her poodle Champagne. Her hobbies include karaoke, quilting and sports. Toni currently resides in Nashville, TN, and can be reached at ToniMDaniels@gmail.com.

 DR. P. KENT SMITH is a visionary community developer who co-founded both LK10 and the Eden Community, where he has found camaraderie in his quest to rediscover God's call to a life of love in our disconnected times.

In his early years, Kent began asking, "How can people in our time actually experience the lifestyle of Joy in community promised by Jesus?" His search for answers led him from studies at York College, through a bachelor's degree in Biology and a master's in New Testament at Harding University, and finally to a doctorate on Spiritual Nurture Systems at the University of Dubuque. Along the way, he led several new and established churches.

In 1991, Kent joined the faculty of Abilene Christian University and began training domestic and overseas mission teams. After a year in Oxford, England in 2002, he became the founding director of ACU's graduate internship in missional leadership, the Missionary Residency for North America (MRNA). In 2008, Kent co-founded LK10 where he serves as overseer and Ecosystem Champion.

Currently, Kent directs ACU's Apprenticeship in Regenerative Culture (ARC). He and his wife Karen have five children and eleven grandchildren. They enjoy gardening, writing, research, travel and their shared work with the Eden Community of coaching students and consulting with new kingdom community initiatives across North America. Kent can be reached at kent.smith@acu.edu

Made in the USA
Coppell, TX
14 April 2020